A Handbook in Theology and Ecology

WWF-UK has been working with religious communities from the early 1980s onwards. Through its religious advisers, the International Consultancy on Religion, Education and Culture (ICOREC), WWF has sponsored new books and approaches in Religious Education; developed new liturgies; published a wide range of resources on the teachings of different faiths on the environment and has involved over two thousand religious communities in the UK in environmental activity.

As part of the WWF/ICOREC programme 'Sacred Land - Rehallowing the Environment of the UK', WWF has assisted in the preparation and publication of this Handbook. WWF itself espouses no religious belief. It does believe that religious communities, with their inherent teachings on the value of nature and their ability to mobilize people, are one of the most important consituencies with which to work to save the environment. It is in this spirit that this Handbook has been developed.

For further details of WWF-UK's wide range of religious and educational publications, please write to WWF-UK, Education and Awareness, Panda House, Weyside Park Godalming, Surrey GU7 1XR. For information on ICOREC's activities in the UK, please write to ICOREC, The Manchester Metropolitan University, 799 Wilmslow Road, Manchester M20 2RR.

Celia Deane-Drummond

A Handbook in Theology and Ecology

SAINT FRANCIS SEMINARY
St. Francis, Wisconsin

SCM PRESS LTD

0 334 02634 2

First published 1996
by SCM Press Ltd
9–17 St Albans Place London N1 0NX

Typeset at The Spartan Press Ltd,
Lymington, Hants
and printed in Great Britain by
Biddles Ltd, Guildford and King's Lynn

Contents

Acknowledgments

In order to write this book I was sponsored by the World Wide Fund for Nature and I have drawn on their expertise in practical environmental action and education. I am also indebted to other members of ICOREC (International Consultancy on Religion, Education and Culture), especially Martin Palmer, Elizabeth Breuilly and Jo Edwards. On behalf of ICOREC, I am grateful to The Manchester Metropolitan University for providing rooms and facilities at its Faculty of Community Studies in support for ICOREC's educational work.

I have had extensive comments and criticisms of the text from academics, ministers, educators and those from development agencies. I have also involved those from a wide diversity of Christian communities at an early stage in design. I am particularly grateful for the insights of Rex Ambler, Jack Hogbin, Janet Morley, Carol Inskipp, John Rogerson, Richard Jones and Stuart Morton, all of whom gave presentations at a working party on theology and ecology in April 1992. The following persons took part in this working party and gave constructive and valuable criticism: George Bebawi, Alexander Belopopsky, Cecily Boulding, Ian Cundy, Eve Dennis, Bernard Farr, John Muddiman, Robert Murray, Ruth Page, Gwynn Williams and Richard Woods. Margaret Barker and Stratford Caldecott were guests for part of the meeting. I am also grateful to many other persons who have made valuable suggestions, in particular Richard Bauckham, Christina Beattie, Jon Talbot and David Gosling. I also would like to express my gratitude to the Ecumenical Patriarch Bartholomew 1 for his invitation to speak at the first Summer Seminar on Ecology and Theology at Halki which, in

1994, focussed on *Religious Education and the Environment*. The stimulation and discussions arising from this seminar helped to contribute to the revision of this text.

I am indebted to the following persons and colleges for taking an active role in testing out sample sections of this book in the context of theological education. These are Richard Higginson at Ridley Hall, Cambridge who liaised with the following staff: Zoe Humphries from Westcott; Revd Martin Cressey from Westminster College and Revd Dr Kenneth Cracknell from Wesley; Christina Le Moigman at Queens' College, Birmingham; John Pritchard at Cranmer Hall, Durham; Christopher Southgate at Exeter University. I have taken their insights and comments into account in the revision of this text. Finally I would like to express my gratitude to Margaret Lydamore of SCM Press for her constructive suggestions and encouragement.

Preface

I have written the handbook so that it is multidisciplinary in approach and orientation. Throughout, I am asking the fundamental question: How can Christian theology engage with ecological concerns in a way which takes into account recent developments in both theology and environmental issues? I am attempting the modest task of giving you the scaffolding and building blocks so that ecological theology can emerge in your particular context. I have constructed the book in a way that quite deliberately leaves gaps for your individual interpretation and comment.

This book is a way of asking certain questions which can then be followed up in particular communities. My hope in giving these broad guidelines is that all thinking Christians will find the task to be within their orbit. Thus, this handbook aims to begin to bridge the gap between academic theology and practical education, ministry and reflection. An ecological theology in the making is, as its name implies, the creative work of the whole human community.

The premise of this handbook is that all Christian traditions have the potential to discover and express ecological concern. I am hoping to encourage anyone interested in theology and the environment to embark on a voyage of discovery in order to explore the wealth of material within their own Christian heritage. I intend to give a few examples by way of illustration, rather than take into account the whole breadth of different Christian denominational positions. The handbook is ecumenical in the sense of accessibility to different churches, while limiting its scope to the Christian theological traditions. My hope is that those from other faith traditions will also find this book informative and useful as part of an ongoing dialogue. I have taken into account religious pluralism, but I have not attempted to elaborate on insights from other faith communities.

I have designed the handbook so as to facilitate the conversation between traditional theology and the 'green' cultural context. You can read it as an individual for your own private reflection and/or as a stimulus for group discussion. If you are involved in theological education in schools, colleges or parochial settings, you will find this handbook a useful resource guide. Within each section I have tried to encourage theological reflection that has three dimensions:

1. *Academic credibility* That is, it takes account of current academic insights and also offers new perspectives that are intellectually rigorous and coherent. An ecological theology should emerge in a way which reflects the norms of each Christian community in terms of its presuppositions about the authority of scripture, tradition and reason and experience. More conservative Christian communities, for example, would give a high priority to the authority of scripture. Others would insist on a foundation in rational philosophical norms. More radical groups would wish to begin with grass roots experience. A more conservative approach puts greater emphasis on the authority of the traditions of the church, which express the history of interpretation of biblical texts. An academically credible view can be argued from any of these basic starting presuppositions.

2. *Educational viability* That is, it reaches students in a way which takes account of recent developments in teaching methods. This applies both in the broad sense and in relation to religious education. The particular stress in teacher-training today is towards encouraging learning through greater participation by students in the learning process. It also seeks to stress integration of practical knowledge with theoretical presuppositions in a way which shares some commonality with training for other vocational tasks such as practical Christian ministry. The interaction between religion and ecology and in particular, between Christian theology and ecology, has been a focus of attention within

school religious education since 1985. I have drawn upon the experiences gained by the teachers and students who have participated in this interaction and this is reflected in the attention paid to educational values and methods. I have also taken into account the developments in adult educational methods, which encourage students to become aware of their own insights and knowledge based on experience. Current religious educational thinking has moved away from the phenomenological approach to religion, encouraging students to observe what is happening, towards an emphasis on the affective nature of religious belief. It looks at the influence, or otherwise, of core beliefs, teachings and stories contained within each faith and culture. It asks the simple question, What difference does it make? What difference does it make to your attitude to nature if you believe in a hierarchical creation with humanity at the crown, rather than a Hindu perspective, for example, which places humanity within a wider framework of beings? It looks at what motivates people to act in certain ways and it seeks to encourage empathy with different positions and beliefs through the use of role play and other educational exercises.

It is from this angle that I discuss the issue of both teaching method, in other words *how* to teach values and beliefs in an open and critical way, and *what* to teach. The emphasis throughout the book on exercises and role play reflects one of the aspects of teaching method. The concern with translation of ideas into actions reflects the concern with what to teach. As such, the book seeks to move forward in an educationally sound way and the sections should be seen as having an internal logic in their progression through issues and in the way the questions and exercises have been selected and placed.

3. *Practical relevance* That is, what real difference will ecological theology make to the life and conduct of both an institution and an individual as well as the future tasks in ministry and leadership? I include questions and points for discussion or action throughout the book which could be taken up in any practical situation. It is often difficult to find creative ways of bridging the gap between academic theology and practical

education and ministry. This handbook is an *aid* in bridging this gap. It also has practical relevance in a second sense by bringing the student up to date on the practical issues of environmental concern which confront us today. The first chapter in this book describes these issues in a way which should be accessible to non-scientists.

I offer guidelines in this handbook as to how you can develop and implement themes in ecological theology. I have subdivided each chapter into a number of specific issues, which you can follow in sequence or you can dip into for particular purposes. I have introduced some basic text under each heading which should give you sufficient information in order to stimulate reflection and/or group discussion. I have highlighted the points for discussion at key points in the text in order to emphasize areas that you can develop further. I have adopted this open-ended approach in order to encourage you to engage in the *process* of ecological theology and to fill out the material in a way that is appropriate for your particular Christian tradition. The bibliography gives guidelines to some of the resources available in the area under discussion. I have tried to include both academic and more accessible books to suit the needs of different groups.

18 December 1995   Celia Deane-Drummond

Chester College

I

Practical Issues of Environmental Concern

1. Global issues in environmental degradation

The purpose of this section is to present a clear picture of the extent of the ecological crisis by highlighting some concrete global examples. It is sometimes tempting to make broad generalizations which miss the complexity of the real issues in the elaboration of Christian ethics. Furthermore, an ecological theology must be contextual, that is take its bearing from the way we have treated and are treating our environment. While the facts I present here are unlikely, in themselves, to lead to concrete action, they are useful background from which we will explore the Christian tradition. It seems to me that we need to strike a balance between exaggerated threats of total devastation (apocalypse) and a pretence that more technology or even religious conversion will solve all our problems (utopia).

One of the more startling aspects of shifts in recent cultural history is a growing awareness of the link between political, economic, social and environmental issues. The so-called 'developed' countries contain 25% of the world's population, but consume 80% of the world's resources. The earth as a whole has a finite carrying capacity.[1] When applied to the human species the carrying capacity of the earth as a whole is more difficult to define. While agriculture and technology can increase this carrying capacity by increasing crop yields, human exploitation of the land in many places extends beyond this natural limit. The results are 'dust bowls, barren lands, devastating floods from deforested hills, the collapse of fisheries, the decline of ancient civilizations'.[2] Between 1960 and 1980 the world's population increased from 3 billion to over 4 billion whereby human demands outstripped natural resources. Another complicating factor in estimating the carrying capacity of the earth is the vast range in standards of living both within and between nations and communities. Recent estimates suggest that if the standard set was that of the richer communities the total world population would have to be halved.

The recent UNCED (United Nations Commission on Environment and Development) 'Earth Summit' at Rio in June 1992 is a good example of how the richer countries were not willing to face up to the implications of the consequences of their past and present economic and political policies. While the global situation is highly complex, especially in areas of political unrest, the temptation to blame the poorest for their mismanagement of land ignores the powerlessness that traps those without means to effect change. In order to equip those in the lower income groups to lead lives which are within the earth's carrying capacity, there have to be changes in economic growth, health care education and employment.

2. Land reform in poor rural communities

Case study

It is the poor farmers in the Third World who most often occupy land which is particularly sensitive to the environmental degradation of the land, that is *land degradation*. If they are pushed on to marginal infertile land by commercial farmers they may have too little crop return to support their families. Out of short-term necessity they may contribute to land degradation by practices such as burning manure and crop residues. In the short term this may contribute to fertility, but in the long term it has the opposite effect. Another harmful practice is allowing livestock to over-graze grass and trees.

The majority of rural families in the poor countries of the South do not own the land they work. They have few reserves to tide over problems such as illness or crop failure. The abuse of power by the landowners is most obvious in those areas where cash crops are grown, or where high input of chemical fertilizer and pesticides reduces the need for labour. More recently, many have argued the case for returning the ownership of land to those who work the land, that is *land reform*. A policy of land reform is bound up with a policy to protect the environment. Poor farmers also lose land through population growth. The greater security offered in land reform means that farmers would be less likely to seek security in having larger and larger families. Hence, giving land back to the farmers would be a stimulus towards lowering the rate of population expansion.

A common strategy of commercial farmers is that of monocultures with accompanying heavy use of fertilizers, machines and pesticides. *Monocultures* are single varieties of crop species, developed through plant breeding. They are much more responsive to fertilizer application, but are also more susceptible to disease. Hence, monocultures require high applications of fertilizers and pesticides, with the accompanying use of heavy machinery. They are also likely to be grown on a large scale. The combination of these pressures leads to soil erosion, loss of tree cover, long-term decline in soil fertility and soil structure. Monocultures also lead to a greater reliance on costly pesticides and a loss of genetic resources, which I will return to again in the section below.

Most peasant farmers, by contrast, practise agriculture which uses *local* crops and does not depend so heavily on chemical fertilizers, pesticides or complex artificial irrigation methods. Hence, their agriculture is ecologically more sensitive compared with monocultures. Alternative, *even more* ecologically sensitive ways of increasing crop yields through application of manures, instead of limited fertilizer use, may not be feasible. Poor families may not be able to afford the long-term strategies of organic farming since organic methods such as composting require both labour and organic fertilizers that may not be readily available.[3] It is now recognized that aid workers need to become aware of the local situation and aim to produce strategies which mix agricultural techniques. This in practice means that *limited* use of fertilizers is encouraged so as to give some short-term benefit while exploring all possible ways of contributing to long-term sustainability.

3. Examples of environmental stress

The examples given below represent a small sample of the current state of environmental damage. The *Atlas of the Environment* gives additional resource material on environmental damage in these and other areas such as population growth, atmospheric pollution, water scarcity and pollution.

(a) Loss of species

By the turn of the century a million kinds of animals, plants and insects are expected to be driven to extinction by human activities. By the year 2050 half of all the existing species could be lost forever. This horrifying reduction in species amounts to a loss of *biodiversity*. This furthermore represents a tragic loss in the genetic potential of the planet. It is estimated that between 5 and 200 species disappear every day. Some species only occur in specific locations, that is they are *endemic* to a particular area of the globe. The Seychelles, for example, has 90 endemic plant species, 81% of which are threatened with extinction.

One of the main causes of extinction is the loss of wild habitats to farming, fuel industry and other human activities. An area of the world's richest source of species are tropical rainforests. According to the *Atlas of the Environment*, published in 1990, there are only about 50% of the mature tropical forests left, that is 750 to 800 million hectares out of an original estimated total of 1.5–1.6 billion hectares. The percentage of the forest left is likely to be even lower than this today. The potential use of plants in medicine is well documented. Drugs extracted from the rosy periwinkle, native to the Madagascan forest, have helped to transform the recovery of children with leukemia from 20% to over 80%. Many of the species will be irreversibly lost before their potential can be explored. So far only a fraction of 1% of the world's plant species have been assessed for potential value for humans.

But from a theological perspective, the value of all species goes far beyond this potential usefulness for humanity. As we will explore further in the chapter on environmental ethics, there are theological and ethical arguments for the preservation of all species, regardless of human interest. The problem is that in general, as far as the scientific community is concerned, the value of species is linked with human interest. Different species now become merely resources for human management. A theological approach can serve to challenge this attitude.

A serious threat to human survival is our dependence on just three species, wheat, rice and maize, to provide half the world's food. Inbreeding in order to increase yields has given these crops a uniform genetic pattern known as a monoculture, which I mentioned above. This has a much higher vulnerability to pests and disease, hence extensive use of pesticides is needed to control damage caused by pests. These pesticides have a damaging effect on the other species in the ecosystem and spread to wide areas through natural river systems. The only effective way to control diseases is by interbreeding with other strains, especially wild varieties. However, it is becoming increasingly difficult to locate these wild varieties as they are to be found in habitats that are rapidly disappearing, usually in the poorer countries of the southern hemisphere. The wild genetic material can be preserved in seed banks, but so far it represents only a fraction of the total seed bank holdings. The ability of such plants to grow in artificial conditions is also restricted.

The same story is true of other crops which have often become crucial cash crops in the Third World. Most of Brazil's coffee traces back to a single tree imported from East Africa via the Caribbean. In 1970 disease struck the crop and spread through Latin America, with devastating effects on the economy. A wild coffee plant from Ethiopia's disappearing forests was used in cross-breeding to prevent a recurrence of the disease.

(b) Land degradation

Land degradation, which I mentioned in the case study above, is also affecting all parts of the globe. As much as 35% of the earth's surface is likely to be turned into a desert, with potential to support life restricted to desert species.[4] People have been creating deserts since the beginning of settled agriculture 10,000 years ago. Nearly the whole of Mesopotamia, lying between the two rivers, Tigris and Euphrates, has become desert, yet over 4000 years ago it was a highly fertile region that supported many thousands of people and was to become the cradle of early civilization. The poor irrigation and over-use of the land rendered it sterile and barren and was one of the main reasons for the collapse of this ancient civilization.

Topsoil takes anything from 200 years to 120,000 years to develop, but it can be lost in a matter of months. Once an area is overused the topsoil turns to dust and is blown away in the wind. Every year 75 billion tonnes of topsoil is lost worldwide. China has one of the worst records on soil erosion. Americans know when the ploughing starts in China because of the dust over Hawaii. Another area where the problem of soil erosion is accelerating is in sub-Saharan Africa, where there are added economic problems. The soils in Africa are especially fragile because they are low in organic matter and clay and erode very easily. Drought, desertification and military conflicts have swelled Africa's refugees to 15 million.

One problem is that while stressed lands can recover a measure of fertility, there is low political motivation to effect change. Ideally this can be circumvented by acting at the local level to effect change. Once the local people are consulted about their problems and are involved in designing the project, there is a much greater chance of permanent success. An example of good practice is Kenya's soil conservation programme aided by the Swedish International Development Authority. The cooperation of the local people led to a set of simple techniques to help prevent soil erosion in a way that farmers could carry out themselves with their own resources. Planting trees around croplands, for example, helps to reduce wind erosion of the soil. By taking simple steps to prevent soil erosion, the overall cost of the project was kept relatively low. There was only limited import of more expensive external assistance. Similar small-scale projects are far more successful than large-scale programmes imposed without proper local collaboration.

Another example is that in parts of West Africa local people are planting kad trees in order to help turn the desert scrubland back into usable land. The land is *reclaimed* for its original purpose. The tree provides shade, buffers the wind and by converting nitrogen from the air into usable nitrogen, known as *nitrogen fixation*, it increases the yield of crops nearby. It has other uses as well. The people can use its pods and seeds as a rich source of protein for cattle and goats and its branches for fuelwood.

- Write out a list of the questions that villagers would raise in discussions over a land reclamation project, similar to the above example. How could their needs be taken into account?

(c) Depletion of energy resources

Global commercial energy use increases each year by 2–3%. I refer here to industrialized societies using energy resources which are traded, such as electricity. According to recent estimates in the *Atlas of the Environment*, oil supplies about half the world's energy, coal one third, mainly for electricity, and natural gas one fifth. By the late 1980s nuclear power was estimated to provide nearly one fifth of the world's electricity. For decades the nuclear industry won popular support because of its perceived efficiency in electricity production. However, once we take into account long-term costs, the real cost of nuclear power is approximately three times more expensive compared with coal. The apparent environmental advantages compared with burning fossil fuels is also offset by the threat of environmental disaster caused by nuclear accidents. Public opposition to building new plants rose after the Chernobyl nuclear accident in April 1986. As a result of the fallout from the accident 31 people died, 135,000 had to be evacuated and between 20 and 40,000 people will die of cancer as a result of increased dosage of radiation. The radiation contaminated foodstuffs both directly and indirectly by entering the start of the food chain. Reindeer feeding on contaminated lichens in Scandinavia, for example, are unsafe for human consumption for many years after the accident. The hidden cost of dealing with the radioactive sections of plants that have been closed remains a burden for future generations.

An indirect effect of energy production is pollution and health risk. Eastern Europe suffers the worst air quality in the industrial world. Nearly 3 million Poles in Upper Silesia in the southwest have to live with up to 1000 metric tons of dust fallout per square kilometre – four times the maximum permitted level. This leads to a 47% higher rate of respiratory illness, 30% more cancers and 15% higher circulatory illness compared with the rest of the country. The awareness of risk at a local level leads to intense concern for environmental issues.

• Discuss the importance of the fear of health risks as a motivating force for environmental concern. Can you think of examples in your own local context?

On average someone in a 'developed' country consumes 18 times more commercial energy than someone in a 'developing' country. We need to encourage greater energy efficiency by using renewable resources such as wind, solar and tide-power, wood burning stoves. There are some signs that this is beginning to happen, as shown by the following examples:

* On Cyprus 90% of homes have solar panels to provide hot water. Over 4 million solar panels are in use in Japan. While solar energy has no polluting effects, there is difficulty in concentrating it so that it can become a source of commercial energy. Israel produced the first solar power station in 1979, using special ponds to absorb the sun's energy in saltwater.

* Electricity for homes in Fair Isle is provided by a giant wind turbine. Ninety-five countries now get electricity from the wind, with California generating 90% of the world total, mostly from windfarms on three mountain passes: Altamount, San Gorgiono and Tehachapi.

* In Cornwall an experiment is being run to make use of heat from rocks six kilometres below ground. In Iceland most of the homes are heated by hot water trapped in rock. If it is hot enough it can be used to generate electricity, as is the case in Larderello, Italy.

* A commercial tide-power plant has operated successfully at the mouth of the River Rance in Brittany since 1967.

Simple societies are driven by human and animal power and fuelled by biomass such as wood, charcoal and dung which are produced and consumed locally and do not appear in a recognized market. Some countries, such as Nepal and Ethiopia, depend on biomass for 90% of their available energy. The problem with this particular approach is that serious deforestation and desertification arises through over-consumption of timber. Here, too, we need strategies for improving energy efficiency through use of small-scale renewable energy resources such as mini hydro-electric projects and solar panels.

Hydro-electric power on a large scale is a mixed blessing because giant dams flood good land or priceless rainforest, trap silt that would fertilize soil downstream and drive people from their homes. The Three Gorges project in China would displace several million people. The absence of atmospheric pollution, such as that caused by burning fossil fuels in order to generate electricity, is a clear advantage of hydro-electric projects. Its potential disadvantages could be overcome by introducing small-scale projects. West Germany now has 3000 small hydro-power turbines. Other small-scale wind turbines are likely to have less technical problems than giant turbines. India plans to produce enough electricity from the wind by the year 2000 to meet the needs of 15 million of its people. Many governments resist using small-scale power generating plants because they are less easy to control than a few large power stations.

• Write out a balance sheet using the guidelines suggested below showing ways in which you consume energy. Keep in mind the following questions: Where does the energy come from? What are the ecological consequences? Are there ways you can begin to change your energy consumption? Suggestions shown in italics.

Type	Energy used/ month	Source of energy, location	Ecological cost
Heating	*Back boiler £25*	*Coal UK*	*High: emission of greenhouse gases*
Lighting	*Electric £5*	*Nuclear UK*	*High: Toxic waste*
Travel	*Bicycle*	*Pedal*	*Low*
Cooking	*Stove £10*	*Gas North Sea*	*High: emission of greenhouse gases*
Food	*Bread £8*	*Wheat USA*	*Medium: transport*
	Canned £15	*Aluminium*	*High*
	Vegetables £20	*Local*	*Low*

(d) Climatic change

Scientists are now in broad agreement that the greenhouse effect is bringing about the greatest and most rapid change in climate in the history of civilization. Carbon dioxide and other gases in the atmosphere act like a glass in a greenhouse, letting the sun's rays through, but trapping some of the heat that would otherwise be radiated back into space. While natural levels of carbon dioxide are needed to keep the climate at a temperature to make life possible, there is considerable evidence that an overall warming of the climate is brought on by human activities which increase carbon dioxide production, such as fuel consumption and deforestation. Every year about 24 billion tons are released, increasing by 750 million metric tons a year. Carbon dioxide accounts for over half the increase in warming of the climate. Other gases which contribute to the greenhouse effect include chlorofluorocarbons (CFCs), methane and nitrous oxide.

As the world climate heats up, rain falls at different times in different places, thereby disrupting crop production. An estimated increase of .3°C per decade results in lower harvests in grain producing countries such as the USA, China and the former Soviet Union. The American Midwest, which helps to feed 100 nations, may see its harvests cut by a third. The new land opening up in Canada as a result of the warmer climate is less fertile, and thus cannot make up for the loss in production in the USA. The countries of the Third World face further loss of usable land through drought and unpredictable rainfall. The change in climate is also expected to contribute to the loss in species, many of which will not be able to spread to cooler areas in order to survive. The Arctic tundra may disappear altogether.

The melting polar caps increase sea levels and flood lower lying coastal areas. A one metre rise in sea level could make 200 million people homeless. Four-fifths of Bangladesh is made up of the delta of the Ganges, Grahmaputra and Maghna rivers, with half the land less than 4.5 metres above sea level. Current research suggests that up to 18% of Bangladesh could be underwater by the year 2050. There are also predictable damaging effects to ecosystems such as coral reefs and mangroves. Almost all the 1,196 islands of the Maldives are less than three metres above sea level at their highest point. Most people living on these islands are only two metres above the sea level. The Cocos Islands, Tuvalu, Tokelau, Kirbati, the Marshall Islands and the Line Islands all face a similar crisis of survival. In all about 300 Pacific Islands are expected to disappear. Our so called 'civilized' industrialization threatens both human and non human life-forms.

- Do you think that certain changes in lifestyle should be enforced by law? What kind of punishments would you impose for environmental crimes?

There is now international recognition of the danger of use of chlorofluorocarbons (CFCs) in their capacity to deplete ozone in the atmosphere. CFCs are compounds which are commonly found in cooling devices such as refrigerators and air conditioning units, as well as aerosols. CFCs released into the atmosphere migrate to the upper atmosphere or stratosphere where they react chemically with ozone and thereby destroy it. Ozone is responsible for protecting human beings and fragile ecosystems against the damaging effects of the sun's ultra-violet radiation. In 1987 over 40 countries agreed the Montreal Protocol phasing out the use of damaging CFCs. Yet it is distressing to realize that according to the US Environmental Protection Agency, even if all ozone depleting chemicals were phased out, it would take a century for conditions in the atmosphere to return to those of 1986.

Similar *irreversible* damage arises in the pollutant effects of other emissions such as sulphur and nitrogen gases. In this case the results are even more drastic in their acceleration of the production of acid rain. The alarming results of recent surveys show that nearly a quarter of Sweden's lakes were acidified and vast areas of forest throughout Europe have been affected by forest death. In all these case studies there is a separation of the source of pollution from the victims of that pollution. In other words those suffering the damage are not necessarily those responsible for the damaging emission.

- Consult your local branch of *Friends of the Earth* or an alternative group to find out if there is a local industry which is polluting the environment.

- Do you notice the effects of this damage?

- Is there any action being taken to curb this practice at the local community level?

- Or at a national political level?

- What are the benefits of this industry for your local community?

- How would you respond if the cost of environmental protection meant that one of your family who worked there lost their livelihood?

- How do you think environmental action can be encouraged at a global level as well as a local level?

- Which of the above examples (loss of species, land degradation, depletion of energy resources, climatic change) did you find most disturbing in terms of potential for ecological damage? Discuss different tactics that could be used to implement change at the international level.

4. Environmental change in local communities

We have hinted at the radical lifestyle changes that need to take place, both as individuals and as communities, if we are to begin to reverse the acceleration towards ecological collapse.

• Make a list of the kinds of lifestyle changes you would be prepared to make in order to live in a way that is more in tune with the environment. How does this list differ from that of your neighbour?

Even though the action of individuals makes little impact in terms of total reversal of trends, there are signs that corporate changes are fostered by individuals and small groups taking responsibility for what has become known as 'sustainable' living, that is living within the earth's resources. I will be returning to the debate over sustainability later.

• Do you agree with the recommendations made by WWF entitled *What on Earth Can I Do?* given in Appendix 2?

In parts of India and Pakistan Christian women have begun what is known as the 'one grain of rice' movement. The idea is that each family puts aside one grain of rice a day, even if they are experiencing hunger and hardship. The pooled rice grains are sold and the money put into a co-operative fund for women. Eventually they have been enabled to buy land which they can work together to grow additional crops.

Different Christian communities across the globe are working towards creating sustainable farming methods. The Benedictines, Franciscans and Trappists have a tradition of high sensitivity to ecological issues in their farming practice. In 1990 the Greek Orthodox Church began the Ormylia project, which promotes organic farming and practice in an area damaged by use of artificial pesticides. This land is under the ownership of the monastery and will become a model for surrounding farms in the area, attracting over 10,000 visitors a year. The Hutterites, Amish and Mennonites base their lifestyle on traditional and sustainable farming practices. This small-scale farming resists use of heavy machinery and relies instead on horse power and community help.

- What kind of role do you think the church should take in environmental issues?

- Is there a difference between recommendations that church leaders can make for their own congregations and those directed at the wider society?

- Should the church community as a whole insist that those in leadership use their influence at a national level?

- Try writing a sample letter to your bishop or church official arguing the case for a greater involvement in environmental action.

2

Ecology and Biblical Studies

1. Genesis 1 and 2 in its historical context

The main purpose of this chapter is to show the possible ways in which biblical studies are relevant to the ecological crisis. The Bible, written many centuries ago, can still speak to our present environmental crisis. One of the most widely-read texts that is relevant to our discussion is the book of Genesis. Genesis was written as a poem to express the faith of the Israelites. It is not a lesson in either the history of creation or the science of the earth's origins. I will try to see the text, as far as possible, in the light of the context of the time, rather than to force it to answer modern questions in a literal way. Ever since the rise of modern science debates have raged over the compatibility of the idea of creation by divine agency with the belief in the purely physical origin of the universe. A particularly controversial discussion was centred round the biological explanation of the evolutionary origin of all species, including humanity. However, the original purpose of the Genesis story was to come to terms with a world that was perceived to be chaotic, rather than to give a detailed explanation of how the world came to exist. The Genesis account is one way of perceiving the world, while the scientific account offers an explanation out of a different modern culture, based on rather different questions. Science does not need to *replace* the Genesis story, it is not the final word about the origin of the world and its continued existence. In other words it is logically possible to believe in scientific explanations without giving them *religious* significance. The Evolutionism of the post-Darwinian era elevated evolution as the explanation of the meaning of our existence. Today there is a tendency for modern physicists to give explanations as if they are the new priests of creation.[1] The opposite extreme to the elevation of science is the Creationism of the fundamentalist churches, which takes the Genesis story as literally true. These debates seem to be far removed from the original purpose of the Genesis story.

- Discuss the alternative attitudes to the origin of the universe. Include a discussion of:
  (i) The agnostic position that the world comes about by pure chance and that evolution provides the fullest explanation of the origin of species. The agnostic debate is around whether the universe emerged from pure chance, or from predetermined natural laws (necessity) or from a mixture of both chance and necessity.
  (ii) A Christian theistic approach aware of the literary context of the stories of Genesis.
  (iii) A Creationistic view that the Genesis account is literally true, and that to think otherwise violates the sacred nature of the text.
  On what basic presuppositions does each view depend?

Bible study: Genesis 1–2

- Read the text and note the picture of the world it encourages. What is the relationship between the Creator and creation?

This text was produced during the Exile, so that the affirmation that all the world is good is an act of faith in a broken world. The Israelites had to contend with a very harsh environment: unpredictable rainfall, storms on the lakes, famines and drought.

The text does not speak of the sun and the moon, but of two 'lights' which is part of the cultic vocabulary of the priests: see Ex. 25.6; 27.20. The idea of lights contrasts with the sun and moon gods of Babylon. This implies that for Jewish writers the whole universe becomes God's temple. The sun and moon are not gods, but simply lights which display the glory of God.

- The purpose of the creation stories was to bring a sense of meaning to the lives of the Israelites in the context of their faith in a Creator God. Try rewriting the stories in the context of the concerns of today.

For example, the understanding of God the Creator and humans as co-creators. The Fall could include more emphasis on the breakdown between the relationship of humankind to the earth.

Note the similarities and differences between the following texts.

Genesis 1 and Genesis 2. In Genesis 1 the land is an island in the midst of waters, which gradually becomes dry through the acts of God in separation and is later inhabited by humanity. In Genesis 2 the land is described as an oasis in the midst of a desert.

In Genesis 1 humanity is created last; this reflects the cult since in liturgical procession the most important figure comes last. Only later do we learn that humanity is male and female. By contrast in Genesis 2 the male is created first to cultivate the earth, followed by the female. In chapter 2 the naming of animals by humans reflects the establishment of order.

Genesis 1–2 and Exodus 14. Similarities between Exodus 14 and Genesis include God speaking and acting so that dry land appears through the separation of the waters. The liberation becomes the omnipotent act of a Creator God. The creation becomes the act of a liberator God who wants not only Israel, but all people to be free.

The Israelites discovered a God who had freed them from slavery in Egypt. God acted in history on their behalf. In the context of the Exile they remembered God's action. God not only acted in history, but created history.

The relationship between humanity and creation follows from the blessing of God and the command in Gen. 1.28 to 'subdue' the earth and 'rule over' every living creature. It is a very significant verse as it follows immediately after God has declared the special place of humankind as those who, *as male and female*, are made in the image of God. Some scholars have sought to link these two verses directly, so that our image-bearing is defined as our task in having dominion over creation. The command to rule parallels that of a shepherd king, whose rule is for the benefit of his subjects. The command to 'subdue' could suggest a forceful submission of the earth to human endeavour. However, exegetical analysis shows that it refers, quite simply, to the *cultivation* of the earth, rather than encouraging any harsh treatment of animals. In the course of the history of Christian interpretation of the texts these words have, at times, been taken to imply a licence to exploit the earth for human benefit. Such an interpretation was encouraged by the seeming success of modern science and humanity's technological innovation and power.

- In the history of interpretation of Genesis the ordering between humans and animals has been interpreted in a hierarchical way. Re-read the Genesis account presupposing an egalitarian rather than hierarchical basis for society. What differences do you find?

Lynn White, a specialist in mediaeval technology, pioneered the idea in the 1970s that Christianity is to blame for the ecological crisis.[2] He argued that Christianity fostered the view that humans are superior to the rest of creation and they have the right to have 'dominion' over it. White believed that the idea of human dominion over creation in Genesis was interpreted by Christians as a licence for human *domination*, fostered still further by the scientific enterprise. A highly influential book by Rachel Carson called *Silent Spring* had appeared in 1962 which showed the devastating effect of the use of pesticides on ecological systems.[3] White's thesis was attractive in seeking to explain the underlying causes behind the ecological crisis. It was also powerful in its simplicity: the root cause of the crisis is the Christian notion of dominion interpreted as domination. However, other biblical scholars have concluded that White's thesis is exaggerated. A detailed investigation of the history of the interpretation of Genesis shows that an interpretation of dominion as *domination* was not as common as he assumed.

White was correct in his belief that the most common Christian interpretation of the place of humans is one of superiority to animals. However, he is wrong in his judgment that this sense of superiority goes hand in hand with an *exploitative* attitude of human beings in relation to creation. In this way White's charge that Christianity is somehow to 'blame' for the ecological crisis is somewhat exaggerated. The text has had a long history of interpretation in an *anthropocentric* way, that is the earth and all the living creatures are there for human need, well before the onset of the ecological crisis.

- Christianity is commonly regarded as *anthropocentric* or human-centred. Can you think of other Bible passages which affirm the value of non-human creation?

The traditional interpretation which insists on the superiority of humans to animals draws on the idea of the unique relationship between humans and God. The uniqueness of the relationship is based on the biblical notion that only humans are made in the *image of God* as described in Gen. 1.27. This has led to the notion of *stewardship*. Human beings are made in the image of God in their role as caretakers or stewards of creation. The question which springs to mind is whether this idea of stewardship is sufficient to counter the exploitative instincts of humanity. Some modern theologians believe that stewardship alone will give too much priority to human interest, as the idea of stewardship suggests management of resources. If we treat the earth as a place to be managed it can more easily be exploited than if we treat the earth and all its creatures as having value in and of themselves. (For a discussion of the relative value of human beings and 'nature' see the chapter on Ecology and Ethics.)

- Discuss the interpretation of Gen. 1.27–28 where it is supposed that human beings are rational and animals non-rational. If we believe that animals are rational and/or have souls, what difference would it make to our attitude and treatment of them?

Nonetheless, the history of cultural ideas shows that the origin of a human-centred or anthropocentric approach is not unique to the Judaeo/Christian creation story. There are strong anthropocentric elements in the philosophical ideas of the Greeks, especially the Stoics. Christian thought emerged from a marriage of Greek and Hebrew thought, which may have contributed to the ambivalence of Christianity towards the natural world. This further weakens the argument that Christianity is in some way directly to blame for the ecological crisis, since an anthropocentric attitude is part of a broader cultural domain. It is true, perhaps, that those strands in the Christian biblical tradition which encourage giving a value to all creation have been neglected or ignored. This is especially true since the Enlightenment, though to place all the blame for the ecological crisis on Enlightenment thinking seems over-simplistic.

A conservative reaction against White's thesis, which is equally exaggerated, is to blame either 'secularization' or 'secularism' as the causes of the ecological crisis. 'Secularization' is the process through which there is loss of significance of religious belief and religious institutional practice, both in the religious and social sense. 'Secularism' often accompanies this process and is the belief that our values should not be based on religion. The temptation to find villains in the story is not helpful and leads to antagonism between different groups. A more positive approach is to highlight those areas in Christian thinking which point to the value of all of creation. Furthermore, encouragement of such value can lead to a great respect for creation. This helps to counter the tendency to treat the natural world as material resources purely for human advancement. An example of a traditional strand in Christian thought which can be rediscovered is the idea of God's blessing to all creation, which we will discuss further in the sections which follow. In this way the Christian approach can help counter an overly-anthropocentric approach. It becomes a way of encouraging a loving and responsible attitude to nature, rather than the opposite exploitative attitude focussed on human benefit alone.

- The anthropocentrism of the traditional interpretation of Genesis was tempered by a theocentric attitude: all creation exists for the glory of God. Discuss the alternatives:
  (i) The exploitation of the earth was encouraged by hierarchical views which stressed human superiority over nature. To counter this we need more egalitarian structures.
  (ii) The exploitation of the earth was encouraged by a loss of the sense of the sacred in all of nature. To counter this we need to recover a theocentric perspective.
  Are these two alternatives compatible?

2. The significance of the eternal covenant after the flood narrative

The ordering of creation described in Genesis reflected right relationships between human beings and God, where the prosperity of the land depends on the peoples' obedience to God's covenant. The obedience of the people refers to social justice and moral integrity as well as a caring, loving attitude to the land itself. This is a common theme in other parts of the Bible.

- Look up Amos and Hos. 4.1–3 and discuss the relationship between God, the Israelites and the land.

The human transgression of the boundaries set by God in the early chapters of Genesis, or the 'Fall' of humanity, led to a disruption of the relationships between human beings, God and the earth. The chapters which follow demonstrate a progressive acceleration of violation of responsibilities between persons and a concurrent wasting of the land. The flood account is rather like a reversal of the creation story where the waters which had been held back by God's decree are now released. All of life perishes apart from those preserved through the diligence and obedience of Noah. After the flood the human race no longer has a benign shepherding role. Instead it commands fear and dread from the animals.

- Compare the role of humanity in Genesis 1 and 2 with that after the flood. Do you think that the account of human behaviour towards creation in the early chapters of Genesis is an impossible ideal?

- Note the places in the first six chapters of Genesis where there is a link between a disruption of human relationships and that with God and creation. For example Gen. 3.17–22, Gen. 4.9–14, Gen. 6.5–8.

There are hints of a *covenant* between God and all of creation expressed in earlier chapters of Genesis where God promises blessing to the animals and humanity (Gen. 1.22 and 1.28). The corruption and inclination to evil in humans incited the anger of

God so that he withdrew his blessing and decreed the flood. Only those creatures protected in the ark escaped death. God now re-affirms that humankind is in his image and promises not to curse creation again on account of the inclination of humans towards evil (Gen. 8.21 and 9.6). The blessing of fruitfulness is renewed (Gen. 8.17; 9.1). God promises *cosmic stability*:

> While all earth's days endure,
> seedtime and harvest, cold and heat,
> summer and winter, day and night,
> shall never cease (Gen. 8.22).

The covenant with creation is formally established in Gen. 9.8–17. God makes a covenant with Noah, his descendants and with all animals, a *promise* never again to destroy the earth by a flood (Gen. 9.8–11). The sign of this covenant is the *rainbow*, a reminder to God and humanity of the promise of God. The relationship between humanity and creation moves from that of peaceful co-existence expressed in Gen. 2.19 to Noah's sacrifice of animals and birds, who live in fear and dread of humans (Gen. 8.20; 9.2). We have moved from an idealistic, paradisal image of the relationship between humankind and creation, to a realistic image depicting things as they are.

We find references to the Noachic covenant in Isa. 54.9–10:

> To me this is the time of Noah:
> as I swore that Noah's flood should no more cover the earth,
> so I have sworn not to be angry with you or rebuke you.
> Though the mountains depart and the hills be shaken.
> my love shall not depart from you
> nor my covenant of peace be shaken,
> says YHWH your compassionate lover (Isa. 54.9–10).

The love promised is *hesed*, which expresses the faithfulness of God in covenant relationship. The eternal covenant of Genesis 9 is associated with faithfulness to the covenant of marriage found elsewhere in the Old Testament, such as Hos. 2.19–20.

• Read Lev. 26.5–6; 26.9; 26.12. You will notice that the promise is for peace *from* animals, rather than peace *with* animals. Compare this text with Ezek. 34.25; Isa. 11 and Gen. 9.

The idea of peace *from* animals described in Leviticus suggests a realistic view of human life as threatened by animals. The idea of peace *with* animals described in Isaiah 11 suggests a visionary view where animals are no longer a threat to each other or to humans. The visionary view contrasts with the realistic view noted in the account of the relationship between animals and humans after the flood narrative.

• How do we reconcile these two pictures of the earth where animals are a threat to or in peaceful relationship with humanity? Discuss this question in the light of the eternal covenant between God and creation outlined above.

3. The Old Testament concept of wisdom as a basis for celebrating creation

The Wisdom literature in the Old Testament reflects the great human questions of life, death, love, suffering, evil, social existence etc. Wisdom brings meaning to these events and so has a timeless quality; it is the art of living a good life. Human beings all struggle to make sense of their suffering. The stories of creation are in themselves Wisdom literature. Wisdom was part of the everyday culture of ordinary people and Wisdom literature reflects this source in popular thought. It was also developed by the scribes who taught wisdom and recorded it in specific books of wisdom. According to later traditions found in books such as the Wisdom of Solomon, the ultimate source of wisdom is divine Wisdom, so the Israelites believed that the way to attain wisdom is through a close relationship with God.

The book of Job recounts a story of one who is subject to unjust suffering. The traditional belief was that suffering is the result of sin, so that the friends of Job tried to make him admit his guilt. Job cries out in despair against these explanations. Eventually God speaks, but does not give Job an explanation of his suffering.

Rather, God overwhelms him with the splendour of the creation. At this Job prostrates himself in adoration.

Bible Study 1: Proverbs 8. 22–31

The book of Proverbs is an excellent source of wisdom literature in the Old Testament. Proverbs 8 is one example of the book's potential usefulness as a resource on the theme of ecology and biblical studies.

The first chapters of Proverbs were probably composed in the Persian period. This passage describes the action of wisdom in concert with the Creator.

Other texts in Proverbs personify wisdom in female categories. *Sophia* wisdom is in striking contrast to the foolish woman (9.13). Wisdom is a prophet (1.20–33); a hostess offering a meal (9.1–6); and a daughter of God (8.22–31). *Sophia* is the feminine divine wisdom. There is some debate as to the source and significance of the idea of personified wisdom. Is *Sophia* a concept gleaned from the ancient Egyptian goddesses of Wisdom, suggesting a separate divine hypostasis? Or is she merely an attribute of God, personified in a colourful way through the idea of Wisdom?

Verse 30 marks an exegetical complexity on the role of Wisdom in creation. In Hebrew only the consonants are written, and in verse 30 we find three consonants making up the root *'mn*, which evokes something solid. In liturgy 'Amen' means 'that is certain'. In this case the verse can either be read with a present participle, *'amon*, the one who founds or who supports, hence architect or master workman; or with the passive participle, *'amun*, one who is carried, or baby, small girl. The alternative readings of Proverbs 8.30 are:

> Then I was beside him, like a master workman (or small girl),
> and I was daily his delight,
> rejoicing before him always.

Bible study 2: The Book of Wisdom

This book is not part of the canon of most Protestant Bibles. The

Roman Catholic Jerusalem Bible includes this book. It was originally written in Greek, probably in Alexandria in Egypt, 50–30 BC. The Jewish community in Alexandria spoke Greek rather than Hebrew, which meant that the Old Testament as a whole had to be translated into Greek. The Greek text became known as the Septuagint (LXX) because seventy scholars were involved in this epic work. Later the Septuagint became the Bible for the early Christians, who often took over its method of interpreting the scriptures.

The book of Wisdom is best studied as a whole as the argument is a developing one, though the following subdivisions may be helpful.

Chapters 1–5: Human destiny The author portrays two different attitudes to life. One is that we are born by chance and we can expect nothing after death. This encourages a thirst for enjoyment at the expense of others. The alternative is that we trust in God and even if we suffer or are persecuted the final reward is that we will live with God.

Chapters 6.1–11.3: Praise of Wisdom The author encourages us to seek the Wisdom of God, she is our friend and companion in our lives.

- Note especially 7.21–30

The author pretends to be Solomon, the wise king, and shows that he owes everything to the fact that he prayed that the spirit of Wisdom would come upon him. Wisdom is the craftsperson of the universe; we read of three times seven divine attributes in 7.22–23, the superlative of perfection.

- What do you understand by the term *image* (eikon in Greek) in Wisd. 7.23–26: A Jew would understand *image* to mean an identity or presence. Compare this text with Gen. 1.26–27.

- What is the role of wisdom towards creation and humanity? Compare this text with that in Proverbs given above.

- Compare Wisd. 7.23–26 with Ps. 104.

4. The significance of the land as an integral component of Old Testament thought

Throughout the Old Testament there is a close interlocking of the people with the land. Both are bound up together in their relationship with God. In Jeremiah 23 and 24, for example, the punishment of the people is connected with the desolation of the land.

- Discuss the significance of the injunction against the abuse of the land in Neh. 5.3–11. See if you can find other references in Leviticus.

A deep pain for the Jewish people during the Exile was the loss of their land, alongside the loss of the monarchy and the loss of the city of Jerusalem. The promised restoration of the fortunes of the Israelites is also bound up with the implicit restoration of their land.

The Old Testament prophets insisted that the land belongs to God, and even though God gave the Israelites the promised land, their right to its ownership can be taken away. God's punishment of the Israelites for profaning the Holy Name is to take away their land (Ezek. 36.21–23). The restoration of the land is only possible in a society that behaves in a just way to all its members. Further, the restoration of the land is for the sake of God's name. In Ezek. 47.22–23 we learn that foreigners, too, have some rights of residence.

- The Exile seemed to reverse the promise of the land which God gave to the Israelites in Exodus. The prophets interpreted this loss as a judgment of God. Discuss the significance of:
  - (i) The restoration of the land assumes right relationships of justice and peace between the peoples and with God.
  - (ii) The exile forced those who suffered this experience to see all land as places where God could be found. Note the struggle recorded in Ps. 137.
  - (iii) Those prophets who predicted that the land would be restored quickly were later denounced as false prophets.

Those who were left behind after the Exile were the poorest of the poor. They lost control over their land as they were subject to the domination and oppression of the rulers. While they still lived on the land their loss of its management was as painful as a physical removal from their homes. The more educated classes were deported. A body of literature emerged in the exiled community which envisaged a drastic destruction of the land followed by a utopian dream of a new heaven and a new earth. There are strands of this so-called apocalyptic thought in the Old Testament, especially Daniel.

- See if you can find apocalyptic strands in Isa. 65. What is the future hope for all creation? See also the comment on Revelation in section 8 of this chapter.

5. The transition to New Testament creation themes

The potential relevance of biblical material for our present context is easier to perceive once we look at ideas about the natural world at the birth of Christianity. In broad terms there were two different ways of perceiving God and the world: the Jewish and the Greek. I noted above that there were parallels between the account of the Exodus where God acted in human history and the stories in Genesis where God created history itself in the creation of the universe. The Jews gave priority to *history* where God was revealed through historical action. Any worship of nature was strictly forbidden because it was associated with foreign Canaanite and Babylonian pagan myths. The Greek culture, by contrast, attached less importance to history and believed their security came through the laws of nature. These natural laws were part of the cosmos and embedded in it. The Greek philosophers were primarily concerned with the study of the universe, which itself was eternal. By contrast, the Jewish philosophers viewed the universe as subject to historical contingency and change. They believed that the world was created as an event that is a gift from God and dependent on God for its continued existence.

- Many cultures of the world see the divine in nature. Do you think that this understanding of the universe or cosmology would be a good way of preventing the exploitation of the earth? How does this differ from the Greek or Jewish cosmologies?

In the biblical narratives there are strands of both Greek and Jewish thought in both the Old and New Testaments, though the influence of Greek culture is stronger in the New Testament. Christian interpretation of Jewish texts is complicated by the significance for Christians of the Christ event. The Christian view emerged from a combination of Greek and Hebrew thought. In general, Christians accepted the idea of natural law taken from the Greeks, but these laws were not divine, eternal or fixed. Rather, the Jewish belief that God created the universe was accepted. This provided the mandate for scientific investigation since the universe was no longer considered divine, either with respect to its laws or in the deified forces of nature in Canaanite thought. According to the Judaeo/Christian understanding, the universe is a gift from God and survives because of its reference to the Creator.

- The idea that God was separate from the world allowed us to carry out scientific investigation. Can you think of some problems which arise if we put too much emphasis on this separation? How might the Jewish belief that creation is a gift from God temper scientific research?

6. The Gospel accounts of Jesus' relationship with creation

The relationship between Jesus and the natural world is not a strong theme in the Gospels. He reaffirms God's care for creatures in the sayings about the lilies (Matt. 6.28–30) and sparrows (Matt. 10.29). He shows himself as Lord of creation in the stilling of the storm (Mark 4.35–41) and in walking on the water (Mark 6.45–51).

- Compare the story of the stilling of the storm with the early chapters of Genesis. What similarities and differences do you find? What does this imply about the role of Christ in creation?

As Lord of creation Christ has the authority to bless or curse creation, as illustrated by his curse on the unfruitful fig tree in Mark 12.12–14; 20–26. The tree, it seems, had no figs, but nor could it be expected to bear fruit as it was not the right season for it! In another case, Mark 5.1–20, Jesus condemns a herd of swine to death to save a man possessed by a demon. We can understand this action a little better than the curse of the fig tree, as in this case he seemed to value a human life more than a herd of pigs.

- Discuss some of the implications of the apparently contradictory relationship between Jesus and creation as illustrated by the story of the curse of the fig tree and the condemnation of a herd of swine.

This somewhat ambiguous relationship between the person of Jesus and the natural world is highlighted by reference to Mark 1.13 which describes the presence of wild animals during Jesus' temptations. Does the reference to wild animals merely signify that he was exposed to the perils of the desert? Or does the idea that Jesus was simply 'with' the animals, without any attempt at domestication or subservience, affirm their independent value for themselves and for God? In other words, it is possible to understand Jesus' time in the wilderness either as an occasion of *peace from* or *peace with* wild animals (see earlier discussion on p. 23).

The messianic lifestyle that the gospel stories portray in Matt. 6.25–34 invites a radical trust in the provision by God for daily necessities of life. There is a parallel between God's provision for the birds of the air and provision for human needs. The message of the story is that if we become too preoccupied by providing for ourselves in our daily tasks we will miss remembering that God is the giver. In the Gospel story Jesus also invites his listeners to consider the beauty of the lilies of the field. God's care for humankind is part of God's open generosity towards all of creation. Those who focus on themselves are never free from their anxiety. In this story Jesus invites his listeners to become liberated from anxiety in order to seek the kingdom of God. This seeking is to become part of knowing ourselves connected with and in solidarity with the rest of creation.

- Read Matt. 6.25–34. List ways in which a modern lifestyle can encourage over-anxiety about human needs. Have we confused needs and wants?

- Read Luke 12.6–8. Here God asserts his care for the sparrows, but also insists that we are worth more than sparrows. Does this suggest a special dignity of human beings compared with the rest of creation?

7. The suffering and future hope for creation in the epistles to the Romans and the Colossians

Bible study 1: Romans 8.18–23

The context of the passage is that of the overcoming of the alienation between God and sinful humanity through the obedience and self-sacrifice of Jesus. The reconciliation is available now to those who have faith in Jesus and become 'justified' or made righteous in God's sight. Those justified receive the Holy Spirit and become adopted as children of God.

The adoption as God's children expresses the coming of the kingdom now, but there is a sense in which the kingdom has not yet come. In theological terminology it is the *eschatological* hope that is both realized now, but not yet in the fullest sense. The future elements of this hope include the justice and righteousness of God coming to the whole of creation. Areas of debate in this passage are:

1. Does the suffering of creation refer just to human beings and not to non-human creation at all?

2. Does the suffering of creation include human and non-human creation, but refer to just those aspects which are connected with human sinfulness?

3. Does the salvation in Christ include the whole of creation in a way which is not linked exclusively to the reconciliation of the damaged human/creation relationship?

- Look up this passage in Romans and discuss the implications for the relationship between humanity and the environment for each of the three alternatives above.

The first alternative is not widely accepted today, that is *creation* is understood to refer to the whole of the cosmos. At the end of the chapter there is reference to hostile cosmic forces, which might suggest that the third alternative is a possiblity. This view emphasizes that the evil that has spread because of the sin of humanity is not the sole cause of the suffering of creation. In other words there are other spiritual forces at work which contribute to the suffering of creation which are not specifically linked to human activity. Nonetheless, the major effects of the ecological crisis can be understood as arising from the results of human sinfulness, that is the second alternative. According to this view the reconciling work of Christ redeems both the effects of the sin of humanity on the human and non-human environment.

Bible study 2: Colossians 1.15–23

This letter was written to a community of mixed Greek and Jewish origin. The city had grown wealthy by the wool trade. However, by the time the letter was written the commercial and social significance of the city was on the wane. The fledgling church was under pressure to conform to the beliefs and practices of their pagan and Jewish neighbours. There is also some evidence that some false teaching had crept into the church, in particular that angels were involved in the creation of the universe. In order to placate the angel's anger the people had to keep strict legal codes. The author asserts strongly that they need only to look to Christ. This passage in particular is one which takes us a little further in understanding the meaning of Christ for creation.

• Read the text several times noting the following points:

1.15: Christ is described as the *image* of the invisible God. This echoes the thoughts of Gen. 1.26–27 which describes humankind as made in *God's image*. God can become human because we bear God's image.

1.15: Christ is described as the *first born* of all creation. The context suggests that Christ is supreme, rather than Christ is the *first* created being.

- Look up parallel texts which show Christ's lordship over creation in Heb. 1.2 and John 1.3

1.16: Christ is described as the one *in whom all things were created*. This idea could mean that Christ is the *instrument* by means of whom all of creation came into being. It also has the sense that all things have their abode in Christ. The heaven and earth are included in the Lordship of Christ. The final part of the verse which says that all things were created through him and in him shows that Christ is both the agent and goal of creation.

1.17: This verse implies the pre-existence of Christ.

1.18: The same word as in 1.15, *first born*, is used here in the relation of Christ to the church. This suggests that the relation of Christ to the creation parallels that of Christ to the church.

- What are the possible implications of this verse as to the significance of creation for Christians?

1.20–23: Christ is described as the means of *reconciling* the disharmony of creation. This reconciliation comes about through Christ's death.

- What are the possible implications of these verses as to the significance of Christ for the future of creation?

The ecological crisis encourages us to reconsider the wisdom of cosmic christology. The words that the author uses suggest that he is drawing on a pre-Pauline text that was used in confessional statements. As in the former text there are areas of scholarly debate about the way the author has modified the text and his particular intention in drawing in the cosmic elements in the celebration of the cosmic Christ. There are at least three possible interpretations of the text:

1. The most straightforward interpretation is that Christ is the foundation of all things (1.16), in which case *all things* is taken to mean the whole *created universe*. The redemption of Christ

(1.20–23) is also understood to include all the created world. I have given this interpretation in the outline above. The idea of cosmic redemption is similar to the third alternative discussed for the passage in Romans 8.

2. An alternative idea is that the author modified an existing hymn to the universe that was part of the philosophy of the time. These modifications draw out the *creative* role of Christ in creation (1.16) but restrict the *salvific* role of Christ (1.20–23) for humanity. This salvific role does include healing the damaged relationship between humankind and creation. In this case the redemption of Christ only refers to human beings and their relationships to God and creation, but not to creation as such. This is similar to the second interpretation of Rom. 8.18–23 that I discussed above. The effect of Christ in reconciling creation is an indirect one, through the salvation of humanity.

- Compare Rom. 8.18–23 and Col. 1.15–23. What conclusions do you reach about the role of Christ in creation?

3. The third possibility is that Christ is the foundation of all things but in this case *all things* refers to humanity *alone*. In this case Christ's creative and redemptive work is restricted to humankind. According to this interpretation the cosmic elements in this passage are included in order to contrast the pagan cosmic view with the Christian one, which is focussed on humankind and the church.

The second and third alternatives require a knowledge of biblical exegesis and literary criticism. Most scholars reject the idea that *all things* is used here in a restricted sense to refer to humanity alone, that is the position 3 above. However, many are uneasy about the first alternative, namely the redemption of creation in parallel with the redemption of humankind. However, even if we adopt the second alternative, the cosmic dimension of Christ's relationship to creation is plain.

8. The future of creation in apocalyptic New Testament literature: Revelation

Bible study: Revelation 21.1–8

The book of Revelation was written in a style which classifies it as apocalyptic literature. Such literature flourished at times of national crises. In the Old Testament, apocalyptic texts are books such as Daniel, Ezekiel and Zechariah. A characteristic of apocalyptic literature is that it presents the earthly creation as that which will ultimately be destroyed. The destruction of creation is portrayed as a catastrophic and sudden event.

The book of Revelation was written in apocalyptic language, most likely by the apostle John when he was exiled to the island of Patmos. The book extends beyond local politics to global issues and beyond global issues to cosmology. There are four possible presuppositions we can adopt when interpreting John's prophecies:

1. The prophecies are simply those which describe future historic events in the particular age in which John wrote the book. This is a view taken by some contemporary theologians.

2. The prophecies describe historic events which will take place at some stage between the time that John wrote the book and the end of history. The prophecies could become explicit in any age. The Reformers accepted this view and tended to identify particular events in their history as foretold in John. For example, they understood the anti-Christ to be the papal authority.

3. The prophecies refer to ahistoric events which will take place far off in the future, at the end of the history, rather than anywhere near the time when John wrote the book.

4. The prophecies are a poetic device, so all attempts to link events with history, either past present or future, are illegitimate.

- Discuss the alternative ways that Revelation can be interpreted outlined in the alternatives 1–4 above. Try to think how you would behave towards creation if you adopted each view. Set up a debate between the different positions. What conclusions do you reach?

The last alternative ignores the actual circumstances prevailing when John wrote to the church, namely the persecution of the churches. Nonetheless, it is clear that while there is some basis in history, the language is that of metaphor and symbol. Jesus Christ, for example, is portrayed as a superhuman character. John uses archetypal themes such as a damsel in distress, a dragon killing a hero, a wicked witch, a rescued bride and a wonderful golden city.

Revelation 21.1–8 describes a cosmic vision that includes the whole social order and the totality of nature.

* Look up parallel texts which describe the idea of a new heaven and earth in Isa. 65.17; 6.22. Compare with Ps. 102.25–26; Matt. 5.18; Mark 13.31, Luke 16.17 and II Peter 3.12.

Rev. 21.3 speaks of God dwelling in a new heaven and a *new earth*. The hidden dwelling of God that we anticipate now on earth will be completed in the new heaven and new earth. We are not told exactly what this new earth will be like, but as in the resurrection of our own bodies we can expect the new earth to bear some correspondence with this earth.

3

Ecology and Celtic Christianity

1. Christianity in Celtic culture

(a) Christianity incorporated into Celtic culture

When Christians first arrived on British soil they were faced with a culture dominated by Celts. The Celtic church grew out of Christian experience in a Celtic culture that was aware of and rooted in the natural world. This close affinity with the natural environment is one reason why Celtic Christianity is of particular relevance to our present age.

Christianity seems to have arrived in Britain remarkably early on in the history of the church. It may have arrived during the reign of Tiberius Caesar, who died in AD 37. Historians of the sixth century have recorded the beginnings of Christianity in Britain. However, their stories have a mysterious, mythological quality. For example, a legend grew up which claimed that the Irish wise men attended the events in Golgotha 'in the Spirit', while at the same time they 'felt the groans and travails of creation cease'.

The native Celtic religion was druidic. The druids were the spiritual leaders of the native Celtic culture and the priests of the sacred oak groves. In Britain the chief druid settlement was the Isle of Anglesey, or Mona. They had special festivals at equinoxes and solstices and sacrificed animals and birds. They also venerated mistletoe, which grew from the oak, and had rites connected with serpents' eggs. The druids in their broadest categorization were poets, civil judges as well as priests. They also practised medicine and were herbalists. They were held in high esteem in the Celtic community. Those druids who were converted to Christianity set about the task of showing how *all of their history* up until this point had been a preparation for the coming of Christ.

The Christian Celtic church took on many of the druidic traditions, such as love of the natural world and poetry, while remaining firmly rooted in Christian orthodoxy. Celtic Christianity successfully transformed a culture, while remaining true to its Christian faith. The gods as taught by the druids could shape themselves into a myriad of different forms: animal, human and divine and were often associated with the land. The gods of classical mythology, by contrast, were astral, such as the sun and the moon gods, rather than earthbound. Even though the Christian Celtic church rejected the gods of the druid faith, they still used some of the legends about their gods in their own legends about the Celtic saints. St Brigit, for example, according to legend, was born in strange circumstances, landed by miracle on the island of Iona and was later brought up by the druids. Her legend attests to her presence at the birth of Christ, where she is supposed to have acted as the midwife. Yet St Brigit was also a *historical* figure, who founded a nunnery and was especially respected for her generosity to the poor. One of the characteristics of the Celtic tradition is this mixture of legend and history.

The deep sensitivity of the Celts for the natural world became part of Celtic Christianity. Christ's death and resurrection became the healing balm for all creation so that the dream of paradise was possible once again. An ancient Celtic legend suggests that Ireland was the site of the original Garden of Eden, so that Ireland shows more clearly signs of a paradise that is now lost. From a historical perspective Ireland remained untouched by Roman rule. It was very rural and was organized in families with tribal chieftains presiding over isolated holdings.

- Discuss the adaptation of Christianity to druid culture. What are the advantages and disadvantages of drawing in elements of pre-existing cultures?

(b) The continuity and discontinuity with the Roman church

Given the depth of spirituality of Celtic Christianity and its accommodation to the native culture, why did it fail to survive? The Celtic church refused to conform to a number of changes in the church taking place on the continent. Above all it was the *form of organization* which was the most significant factor affecting the future survival of the Celtic church. The Roman church had no qualms about adopting a Roman system of organization and hierarchical structure. For the Roman church, the source of authority was strictly through the bishops. The Celtic church, by contrast, gave organizational power to local abbots and some female abbesses and preferred spiritual guidance to be through a soul-friend. The result was that each monastery had considerable autonomy and individuality, with rites and customs adapted to the local area. While the bishops had ritualistic authority, they had no real power.

- What are the advantages and disadvantages of a locally-based church organization? Do you think the same tensions exist today between the universal church and local variations?

- In the Celtic church female abbesses had considerable power and authority. Discuss the possible links between Celtic affirmation of nature and women.

It was the lack of uniformity in Celtic Christianity which irritated the Roman church. Pope Gregory the Great commissioned Augustine, prior of a monastery in Rome, to conduct a mission to the Kentish tribes of Southern England. The influence of Augustine of Canterbury gradually spread further north, though he met with considerable resistance from the bishops and abbots of the Celtic church. A further point of controversy was the calculation of the date of Easter which in the Celtic church closely resembled that of the Eastern church. Eventually, in 663 King Oswy of Northumbria called a synod at Whitby to discuss the date of Easter. This synod was to prove momentous for the future of the Celtic church. Although it was not on the official agenda, the debate at the synod became one of the status of Celtic

Christianity itself. The Roman view prevailed and this marked
the demise of the official influence of the Celtic church in Britain.
The Celtic communities dispersed, many taking refuge in remote
islands in Scotland.

- Read the account in Bede of the Council of Whitby in 663. Put your
  findings in the form of a drama.

- Rewrite a short history of the church imagining the synod had
  voted in favour of Celtic Christianity. Discuss the implications for
  today.

The freedom for individual expression more characteristic of
the Celtic church has become much more possible in more recent
times in the Roman Catholic church since the second Vatican
Council which met in 1962. A significant proportion of the 2,500
bishops and other dignitaries who met for this council were of
Asiatic or African origin. This may have contributed to a move
away from the rigidly centralized structure towards a greater
openness to lay participation in the life and liturgy of the church.

- What are the possible threats to a more open church structure?
  Does openness necessarily lead to fragmentation?

2. Are asceticism and love of nature compatible?

The stories and legends associated with the Celtic saints describe
remarkable feats of devotion and ascetic practices. Their love of
God and of the natural world was complementary, they loved the
creatures that God created. The practice of asceticism helped to
focus their minds and hearts on the love of God. These saints were
determined to express their faith through simplicity of life and
self-denial. This self-denial of material goods brought them in
close contact with the natural world and heightened their
appreciation of its wonders and beauty. In other words their
asceticism, at its best, was not a romantic escapism or a denial of
the worth of the goodness of creation. Rather, it was an
affirmation of the love of the Creator and all creatures. This
tradition continued in the lives of later saints such as St Francis of

Assisi. Their devotion to long hours of fasting and prayer, often in harsh circumstances, is also characteristic of Eastern ascetic Christian mystics. Stories about St Kevin, for example, tell how he used to lie at night on hard stones near Lake Glendalough. He ate nothing but sorrel and nettles for seven years and for many years had no contact with other humans. He fasted every Lent, going without food for forty days.

Is deliberate self-denial of bodily comfort compatible with love of the natural environment? I could argue that some of the extremes to which the saints practised their asceticism *was* negative in terms of its potential failure to affirm a holistic appreciation of all of human life: body, mind and spirit. However, one of the purposes of the more extreme asceticism of the Celts was a surrender of the needs of the body in order to come closer to the *suffering* of Christ. In drawing deeper into Christ's suffering the Celtic saints experienced in a powerful way the reality of his resurrection. This gift of the Holy Spirit allowed them to see all of creation as a gift and as a reflection of God's glory, even if marred by human sinfulness. At its best, then, asceticism *could* lead to a positive affirmation of the natural world. Yet there does remain a danger that asceticism promotes a somewhat masochistic focus on suffering. While self-denial is useful in a limited way as a means to restrain greed and over-indulgence, it seems to me that deliberate self-punishment in order to re-enact the sufferings of Christ is a somewhat precarious path to follow.

The theology of the Celtic church was basically orthodox and had much in common with the Roman church, though there was a much greater emphasis on scripture and asceticism. It drew its inspiration from the mystical tradition of the Eastern church of Egypt and Syria. The doctrine of God was fully Trinitarian. Creation came into being by divine will and its original purpose was to reveal the character of God. This *sacramental* role of creation was marred by human disobedience. The Celtic tradition was that through Christ the original purpose of creation is possible once more.

They insisted that the world was created good and the spiritual and material worlds were not separate but a single unity. This is a particularly relevant insight for us today where we have lost the sense of the spiritual in the material world. In Celtic Christianity God's power, God's spirit and God's grace is visible everywhere in the natural world and in our dealing with it for those who have eyes to see this truth.

- Discuss the relevance of the Celtic affirmation of the goodness of creation in a consumer society. What are the effects of supermarket packaging etc. on the relationship between us and the source of these goods?

- How do you think that Celtic saints might justify the practices of self-denial in the light of their affirmation of the unity of the material and spiritual?

The Western theological tradition, following Augustine of Hippo, separated uncreated grace, that is God's personal presence or Spirit, from created grace, that is the state of grace produced in God's creatures. The Celtic approach did not make any such distinction. For them grace means God's life-giving presence to all and within all things, both personal and impersonal, spiritual and material.

- How might our attitude to the environment be affected if we separate God's uncreated grace from created grace, following Augustine?

This unity of the spiritual and material worlds allowed the Celtic Christians to find God in all things. The love of God and neighbour is in everyday events and actions such as sleeping, walking, eating and journeying, sowing and harvesting. This applies to the city as well as the rural community. This is especially important in our culture which has become increasingly urbanized. If we see God in all of creation, the work of human hands has the power to express the presence of God. The time spent in hermitage was in preparation for missionary activity in the city.

- Imagine a Celtic saint has reappeared in a modern city. How might this saint respond to the vocation to find God in all things?

- In what ways could a city be designed so that it takes into account the need for a close relationship between humanity and creation?

The era of the Celtic church was also a time when Christians took up the practice of being pilgrims or wanderers for Christ. These Celtic pilgrims were not venturing forth to a holy place, but chose to suffer the loss of all that was familiar in home and family for the sake of bringing Christ to others. The traditional name for this practice of pilgrimage for Christ is 'White Martyrdom'. This differs from 'Red Martyrdom' where the saint's life was lost for the sake of Christ. This single-minded devotion to Christ prevented their love of the natural world in some way replacing Christ as the focus for their spirituality. They were 'nature' mystics in the best sense of still being rooted firmly in Christ-centred worship. 'Nature' is defined here as the natural non-human environment. It is easy to forget this explicit Christian missionary element.

- Discuss the trend of some contemporary creation-centred spirituality where there is a replacement of Christ-centred worship with 'nature' worship. What corrective does Celtic Christianity offer?

Related to this ideal of self-surrender for Christ is the practice of becoming separate from the world and living a period of life dedicated to prayer in solitude. The Celtic church is remarkable for its strong discipline and austerity, paralleled in the Eastern ascetic tradition. The tradition of island sanctuaries grew up; the most famous in Britain are those on Iona, Lindisfarne, St Kilda. Some of these buildings are quite spectacular: on Skellig Michael in Ireland there is a collection of so-called 'beehive' cells which rise seven hundred feet above the Atlantic, built on sheer rock. This rock is seven miles from the mainland. The 'beehive' cells have no opening except a door and sometimes a slit for ventilation.

The hermits were not totally alone in their cells. They shared their room with a soul-friend or companion. The beehive cells were often situated close to a monastery and the monks used either a chapel built near the cells or the one in the monastery. The Celtic Christian tradition of friendship is important as it counters the otherwise somewhat harsh tradition of fasting and self-denial.

- Discuss ways in which you think that the practice of having a soul-friend can be applied to contemporary society.

While the motive of the Celtic saints was ascetic, it often led them to places of outstanding natural beauty. Their love of poetry and scholarship gave them an outlet to express their love of God which they experienced in the created world. They seldom wrote straight 'systematic' theology, but allowed poetry to be the medium in which they could express the wisdom of God:

> Learned in music sings the lark
> I leave my cell to listen
> His open beak spills music, Hark!
> Where heaven's bright cloudlets glisten
> And so I'll sing my morning psalm
> That God bright heaven might give me
> And keep me in eternal calm
> And from all sin remove me.

> an unknown author cited in R. Flower (ed),
> *The Irish Tradition*, Clarendon Press 1947, p. 47

- Compose your own poem in the Celtic tradition, using your daily experience as a basis for reflection.[1]

3. The Celtic understanding of the natural world as expressed in the lives of the saints

The Celtic tradition is replete with stories about the lives of Celtic saints. I will draw on the examples of Patrick, Columba and Pelagius in so far as their stories relate specifically to their understanding of the natural world. Their lives offer particular examples of how their contact with the natural world affected their particular understanding of Christianity.

(a) St Patrick (b.c.387)

St Patrick was born in Scotland or Wales. As a young boy of sixteen he was kidnapped and became a slave in Ireland. He was forced to be a shepherd, which exposed him to the wild natural elements. He described how his own faith grew in the context of his close communion with the natural environment. He escaped and became a Christian monk. He was eventually sent to Ireland as a missionary bishop. He identified with some of the traditions of the druids, but remained Trinitarian in his Christian beliefs. The success of St Patrick's mission to Celtic Ireland may largely be accredited to his willingness to adapt the indigenous beliefs to Christian practices. Nonetheless, St Patrick was very firm in his rejection of any elements of druid religious worship which were in opposition to Christianity.

St Patrick encouraged and strengthened the Celtic church in Ireland that later spread to Iona in Scotland and from Iona to Lindisfarne. These centres of Celtic Christianity gathered round charismatic leaders and saints of the church such as Columba, Aidan and Cuthbert.

St Patrick was once asked who the Christian God is, and he replied:

> Our God is the God of all, the God of heaven and earth, of sea and river, of sun and stars, of lofty mountain and the lowly valley, the God above heaven, the God in heaven, the God under heaven; he has his dwelling round heaven and Earth and sea and all that in them is. He inspires all, he quickens all, he sustains all. He lights the light of the sun; he furnishes the light of the light; he puts springs into dry land and has set stars to minister to the greater lights.

- What does the above extract tell you about St Patrick's theology of creation? His understanding of God? His missionary tactics?

Legend has it that St Patrick wrote his famous hymn for protection known as *St Patrick's Breastplate* while he was escaping from the region of Tara in Ireland. Those who lay in wait for him saw eight deer and a fawn with a white bird on its shoulder run past. This is said to be Patrick and his eight companions. Although the earliest known written version of the hymn dates from the sixth century, it is commonly believed that the original version of the hymn was written by Patrick at this time. Hence the poem is also sometimes called 'The Deer's Cry'.

The hymn signals the personal awareness of the love of Christ and a reassurance of his presence that is an integral part of Celtic Christianity. Christ is present as a protector, summoned just after the invocation of the Trinity at the beginning and end of the hymn. There is no sense in which Christ is set in opposition to the Father. Notice the rhythm of each stanza as it builds through the hymn.

> I arise today
> Through a mighty strength, the invocation of the
>   Trinity,
> Through belief in the threeness,
> Through confession of the oneness
> Of the Creator of Creation.
>
> I arise today
> Through the strength of Christ's birth with his baptism,
> Through the strength of his crucifixion with his burial,
> Through the strength of his resurrection with his
>   ascension,
> Through the strength of his descent for the judgment
>   of Doom.
>
> I arise today
> Through the strength of the love of the Cherubim,
> In the obedience of angels,
> In the service of archangels,
> In the hope of the resurrection to meet with reward,
> In the prayers of patriarchs,
> In prediction of prophets,
> In preaching of apostles,
> In faith of confessors,
> In innocence of holy virgins,
> In deeds of righteous men.

I arise today
Through the strength of heaven;
Light of sun,
Radiance of moon,
Splendour of fire,
Speed of lightning,
Swiftness of wind,
Depth of sea,
Stability of earth,
Firmness of rock.

I arise today
Through God's strength to pilot me:
God's might to uphold me,
God's wisdom to guide,
God's eye to look before me,
God's ear to hear me,
God's word to speak to me,
God's hand to guard me,
God's way to lie before me,
God's shield to protect me,
God's host to save me,
From snares of devils,
From temptations of vices,
From every one who shall wish me ill,
Afar and near,
Alone and in a multitude.

I summon today all these powers between me and those
　　evils,
Against every cruel merciless power that may oppose my
　　body and soul,
Against incantations of false prophets,
Against black laws of pagandom,
Against false laws of heretics,
Against craft of idolatry,
Against spells of women and smiths and wizards,
Against every knowledge that corrupts man's body and
　　soul.

Christ to shield me today
Against poisoning, against burning,
Against drowning, against wounding,
So there come to me abundance of reward.
Christ with me, Christ before me, Christ behind me,
Christ in me, Christ beneath me, Christ above me,
Christ on my right, Christ on my left,
Christ when I lie down, Christ when I sit down, Christ
    when I arise,
Christ in the heart of every man who thinks of me,
Christ in the mouth of every one who speaks of me,
Christ in the eye of every one that sees me,
Christ in every ear that hears me.

I arise today
Through a mighty strength, the invocation of the
    Trinity,
Through belief in the threeness,
Through confession of the oneness
Of the Creator of Creation.

> Kuno Meyer's translation in
> *Selections from Ancient Irish Poetry*, 1928

- What role does creation have in this poem?

- The invocation of 'nature' parallels the invocation of the saints, the faithful departed. Discuss what this implies about the relationship between the natural and spiritual world.

- The poem invites protection against the spells of women, smiths and wizards. As I mentioned earlier, women had much greater authority in the Celtic culture and were known for their wisdom. This ability could be used for druid practices that clashed with the Christian faith as well as those practices which could be accommodated within it. In this context do you think that this poem is affirming all of creation, including women?

(b) Pelagius (c.360–c.430)

Pelagius is thought to have been born in Wales or Ireland. He was well educated and went to Rome initially to study law. He was the first known British theologian who wrote extensive Bible commentaries. He was a man of considerable intellectual and religious force, but he was also a highly controversial figure in the Roman church. Roman historians write of him in derogatory terms, making scathing comments on his huge bulky build and slow gait! However, until 415 he was accepted by the church as fully orthodox.

Pelagius' theology has a curiously modern ring with its emphasis on *human* responsibility for sin. If we apply his ideas within our contemporary context he would be harsh in his assessment of the *human* responsibility for the ecological crisis. However, he would also insist that we have the potential to change our situation with the help of God's grace. Pelagius argued that a human life free of sin is only possible by sheer gift of God. He stressed *human responsibility* in co-operation with the action of *God's grace*. Pelagius never denied the grace of God in human nature. In common with the Eastern church he stressed that sin was the responsibility of human beings coming from individual choice. He refused to accept the dogma that Augustine of Hippo preached on 'original sin'. Augustine and subsequently the Western tradition developed the concept of 'original sin', that human nature since the 'fall' of Adam was corrupt. Augustine's views could be interpreted in such a way as to lead to the conclusion that a newborn baby is forever condemned by God until baptism.

- How might the idea of original sin affect attitudes to the ecological crisis? Is the crisis inevitable?

A positive application of Augustine's teaching for today would be to stress the consequences of sinful action against the natural world for future generations. Pelagius' teaching, with its stress on human responsibility, could suggest that perfection is possible through human effort.

- How might a modern Pelagian respond to the ecological crisis?

Perhaps Pelagius' optimistic anthropology is an important

corrective to the more extreme pessimistic elements implicit in Augustine's thought and strands from both writers help us to envisage a more realistic anthropology.

- Set up a debate between an Augustinian and Pelagian in the modern context of the role of humans in ecological crisis.

Pelagius' views about the possibility of a sinless life were challenged by Augustine in 413. Augustine believed that Pelagius was heretical because he seemed to suggest that salvation was possible by human effort. However, Pelagius' ideas were about *discipleship* and living out the Christian life, rather than the means of salvation. At first Pope Innocent I acquitted Pelagius of the charge of heresy in 415, but later issued a conditional condemnation. The new Pope, Zozimus, was an Eastern Christian, much more sympathetic with Pelagius' views and he declared Pelagius as fully orthodox. Later the African church eventually pressurized Zozimus to change his mind, though this document has been lost.

This brief excursus into the history of the Pelagian controversy is important as it shows how ambiguous were the terms on which he was condemned. Today it is unlikely that a charge of heresy would be made on such grounds. It seems to me that his theology is of particular relevance to our present ecological crisis.

Pelagius is also important for his characteristically Celtic approach to the natural world. His writing was very popular in Celtic Britain and was second only to the influence of the Eastern church on Celtic Christianity. His approach is thoroughly Trinitarian and his Confession of Faith bears a close resemblance to that of St Patrick. He believed that there is a unity of action in human freedom and God's grace: both are gifts from God. His concern for public morality and social justice may have contributed to his being ostracized by the Roman church who were anxious to win the favour of imperial courts. The challenge of Pelagius to the social and public conduct in the life of the community is a particularly important reminder to us that Celtic Christianity had *public social* consequences as well as influencing the *private devotional* life of individuals. His concern for social justice has a contemporary ring. The tendency to demand ecological action without seeking justice in the human community is one of the reasons why many of those in the poorer countries of the Third World have been hesitant in their acceptance of the urgency for action in environmental issues. As we will see later on in chapter 8, on Ecology and Politics, the two areas of social justice and ecological action make sense if they are considered together as part of the one crisis.

Pelagius was thoroughly committed to the study of scripture and finding the wisdom of God in the written word and the natural world. For Pelagius and the Celtic church Christ came to liberate a world held in bondage to sin. Christ in Celtic thought comes to scatter dark forces so that the original light of the natural environment is revealed. This contrasts with the idea that Christ comes to replace the light of the natural environment with a different light. The Celtic view of the natural world was above all realistic. It recognized the damage done to creation through human sinfulness, but insisted that Christ as cosmic lord came to liberate creation from her bondage. The idea of Christ as liberator is popular today, and the concern to liberate human beings from oppression would be in tune with Celtic thought.

St Columbanus (543–615) followed in the tradition of Pelagius. The following are some of his sayings:

> Let us be careful that no image but that of God takes shape in our souls.
>
> The wise person meditates on the end of his or her life.
>
> The person to whom little is not enough will not benefit from more.
>
> Be hard among pleasant things, be gentle among harsh things.
>
> Let the heart have its reins firmly on the tongue.
>
> The ones who trample on the world trample on themselves.

- Discuss the implications of each of these sayings for the ecological crisis.

(c) St Columba (c.521–597)

Early in his life St Columba spent most of his time writing poetry, but he eventually became a monk. According to legend, through an act of penance he journeyed to Iona, a small island off Mull on the West Coast of Scotland.

Columba became known as a person of knowledge, of power and of God. He is described as one who lived in close communion with the natural environment and the angels. Legend has it that those who came near his church often saw the whole building filled with celestial light. Other stories tell how he won the affection of creatures and animals. At his approaching death the white horse belonging to the monastery buried his head in the saint's lap and shed tears, foaming at the mouth in distress. Columba, in common with other Celtic saints such as Cuthbert, Kevin and Ciaran, had a close friendship with and affection for animals, birds and all of creation, as the following psalm by Columba illustrates:

Delightful I think it to be in the bosom of an isle, on the peak of a rock, that I might often see there the calm of the sea.

That I might see its heavy waves over the glittering ocean, as they chant a melody to their Father on their eternal course.

That I might see its smooth strand of clear headlands, no gloomy thing; that I might hear the voice of wondrous birds, a joyful tune.

That I might hear the sound of the shallow waves against the rocks; that I might hear the cry by the graveyard, the noise of the sea.

That I might see its splendid flocks of birds over the fullwatered ocean; that I might see its mighty whales, greatest of wonders.

That I might see its ebb and its floodtide in their flow; that this might be my name, a secret I tell, 'He who turned his back on Ireland'.

That contrition of heart should come upon me as I watch it; that I might bewail my sins, difficult to declare.

That I might bless the Lord who has power over all, Heaven with its pure host of angels, earth, ebb, flood tide.

That I might pore on one of my books, good for my soul; a while kneeling for beloved Heaven, a while at psalms.

A while gathering dulse from the rocks, a while fishing, a while giving food to the poor, a while in my cell.

A while meditating upon the kingdom of heaven, holy is the redemption; a while at labour not too heavy; it would be delightful.

Translation by Kenneth Hurlestone from
A Celtic Miscellany, Jackson Penguin 1951

• Notice, in particular, the sheer delight in the natural world and the affirmation of creation's goodness that is so characteristic of Celtic thought.

St Columba's monastery on Iona became a centre for learning, prayer and refuge. King Oswald from Northumberland spent some time here while his kingdom was in disarray. Later he asked for a bishop from Iona to come to Northumberland. St Aidan arrived, and founded the Celtic monastery on Lindisfarne which was to become another centre for Celtic Christianity in Britain.

The unofficial influence of Celtic Christianity survived in the lives of saints such as St Cuthbert of Lindisfarne, who was from the Roman church, but is still Celtic in his love of the natural world and asceticism. The Lindisfarne Gospels, written to commemorate his death at the end of the seventh century, are remarkable for the intricacy of their Celtic design and art work.

• Discuss the following statement by historian H. J. Massingham:
'If the British (*ie Celtic*) church had survived, it is possible that the fissure between Christianity and nature, widening through the centuries, would not have cracked the unity of western humanity's attitude to the universe' (H. J. Massingham, *Tree of Life*, Chapman and Hall 1943).

4

Ecology, Women and Christian Community

1. The challenge of feminist theologians to traditional theology

Christian feminist theology includes a wide spectrum of views which seek to reform to a greater or lesser extent different aspects of the Christian tradition. According to this view the Bible was written by men who lived in a particular culture that stressed the authority and dominance of a father figure, or *patriarchy*. A patriarchal culture is associated with an ordered structure of relationships in a hierarchical way, with the father at the head. The theology which emerged as a reflection on the scriptures was almost entirely the creation of men. God is described in male categories, for example as a king, shepherd, father and always with the masculine personal pronoun. Feminist theologians insist that theology as created by women needs to take a different shape. The emphasis is now on theology emerging from the *experience* of women within egalitarian social arrangements. In other words, it is not simply a replacement of patriarchy by *matriarchy*, where the mother figure is dominant, but a re-placement of hierarchy by *egalitarianism*.

The creation of feminist theology by women coming from experience is not an exclusive one. All theologians, male and female, could take the experience of egalitarian social structures as a starting point. The difference between traditional theology and feminist theology is that feminists are convinced that traditional views presuppose a patriarchal social structure which oppresses women. Furthermore, traditional theology begins with theoretical doctrines, rather than experience in community. If male theologians adopt the latter view they become feminist in their attitude. We are not dealing so much with differences in thought caused by *biological* differences, but differences in attitude coming from *social conditioning*.[1] Just as it is possible for men to take up a feminist perspective, so it is possible for women to take up a patriarchal perspective. A sharp critique by conservative women and men is that feminists do not recognize the experience and views of ordinary women who are quite content to be part of social structures where males take responsibility and are dominant. They argue that the views of feminists come from the experience of a liberal middle-class elite. A feminist reply to such criticism is that those women who conform to this attitude are failing to express their full potential. If sexist attitudes prevail it is always at the expense of women. If the sin of men is to be arrogant and proud, the sin of women is over-submission and a failure to be assertive. It is also questionable that feminist theology represents the writing of just middle-class Western women. Those women writing from the African, Latin American and Asian contexts are also very significant in giving a voice to those speaking out of their own experience from very different cultural contexts. In other words, feminist theology is much wider than the view of a middle-class elite in Western culture.

- Do you believe that men and women see the world and relationships in different ways? What are the implications of this?

Some feminist writers argue that hierarchical social arrangements of any kind are unhelpful, both in themselves, and as a context in which to think about God. As a first step in *re-imaging* God we need to think of God in female categories as well as male categories. Many feminist writers stress the female nature of God in order to compensate for an overemphasis on male images in the past. I will return to this point in section 2 below. The complaint of feminists is that the views of half of humanity have not been acknowledged in the fundamental questions about the way we understand who God is and who we are in relation to creation. A common thread in more conservative feminist writings is a desire to re-examine the biblical material in a way which gives greater prominence to women's experience of relationships. The relationships with other humans also extends to include the relationships with the earth. Included and embedded in the re-writing of theology is a desire to place more emphasis on human experience than is rooted in the material, earthly world. The concern, then, of feminist writers is that Western culture has been dominated by male social structures and male values which encourage detachment and separation, rather than involvement and integration. Some more radical feminists believe that Christianity is bound up with a patriarchal culture to such an extent that we need to replace it with another religion altogether. More moderate feminist writers argue for a reformulation of Christianity. I will be presupposing this more moderate view in the discussion which follows.

We need to ask the question: What would Christian theology look like as written by women? There is a desire to affirm women in a way which helps them to speak and achieve autonomy and freedom from male domination. For feminist theologians the autonomy of women means focussing on creative images of the whole of humanity. Both men and women as made in the image of God have joint responsibility for the care of the earth. *Eco-feminists* put particular emphasis on the current damage to the environment which they believe is bound up with sexist attitudes. As men have had the power and responsibility for what happens in society, feminist theologians tend to blame men for the ecological crisis. A male domineering attitude to women encourages a similar attitude to the earth. It is the association of women with the earth and irrationality and men with rationality and spirit that encourages men to dominate both women and the earth. The injustice towards women is mirrored in irresponsibility towards the earth. In other words the dominance of men over women for *eco-feminists* mirrors the domineering attitude of men towards creation. The logical conclusion is that if men and women are to repair the damage to the earth we need to overcome first a sexist attitude in men. Another significant issue is that the questions of justice and models of development are part of the feminist theologies emerging from the Southern contexts.

- Explore the connection between our attitude and action in our relationships to each other and the earth.

- Discuss the possible link between male domination of the earth and male domination of women.

- Is it necessary to counter prejudice and discrimination against women first, before we counter aggression against the planet?

The common thread in feminist theologies from both the Northern and Southern hemispheres is to make the starting point for theological reflection the experience of relationships. This rootedness in experience is above all a concern for a just communal life. The experience of life of ordinary women is commonly that dedicated to sustaining relationships within the family unit. In other words self-determination is found within the context of relationships, rather than one that is individualistic and narrowly rationalistic. We can extend this experience so that it is used for the benefit of the wider human community and a deeper sensitivity to human relationships with all creatures. It is this wider horizon that feminist writers argue is essential if our society is to become more fully human. In the past the emphasis on competition and separation into discrete individual specialisms has led to an alien technological culture that has not recognized sufficiently the importance of human relationships. The gift of women to the wider community is to redress the balance and encourage both men and women to work for more harmonious social relationships. In other words the recognition of sociality within the human community is part of a wider recognition of the sociality of all things. In this way mutual relationships are not narrowly defined, but both ecological and cosmological.

The theological significance of these insights is that for many feminist theologians it becomes impossible to perceive God in the same way as traditional orthodoxy which they believe emerged as talk about God for men and by men. In the section which follows we will explore how these insights have clashed with more traditional views.

- Using some central creation themes such as the biblical story of the creation of the world, or the coming of Christ to earth, explore some of the ways in which these stories could be re-written from a feminist perspective. Would such a reformulation convince the more radical feminists who believe that Christianity is inevitably patriarchal?

2. Thinking about God in social and feminine categories

The traditional approach to an understanding of God is one which stresses both God's otherness to creation, that is God's *transcendence*, and God's nearness to creation, or *immanence*. As long as these two aspects of God's nature are held together in paradox the value of creation is ensured.

- What are some of the advantages in understanding God as in some way apart from us or transcendent? For example, how does this affect our sense of security both now and in the future?

- What are some of the advantages in understanding God as in some way involved with us or immanent? For example, how does this change our attitude to nature?

There are problems, however, when we forget the immanence of God and concentrate on God's transcendence. One of the legacies of the Enlightenment attitude to nature, following Descartes, is a belief that the world is like a machine. This mechanistic approach for the sake of scientific study can become a way of seeing the world. The concept of transcendence conveniently removes God from participation in the mechanistic world. If we think of the world as a machine it seems to give us permission to change it to suit human need. The exploitation of the earth seems acceptable if it is called 'management of resources for human benefit'. (For a further discussion see chapter 8 on Ecology and *Gaia*.)

There are various alternatives to counter the over-concentration on God's otherness:

1. First we could simply insist that God is immanent in creation as well as transcendent. These two aspects of God's nature are complementary.

2. We could conceive of God as being shaped in some way by the world. This is the view favoured by more liberal theologians, loosely described by the term 'process' theology. The particular influence of process theology in shaping an understanding of God is to stress the twin ideas of God's passibility, that is the ability to suffer, and God's mutability, or ability to change. In other words God in some sense shares in both the suffering and creativity of the world. The idea of God's immutability is restricted to qualities such as God's love or God's faithfulness. Thus the God of history and creation has an open future, one that is partly determined by creation. In this way human beings are co-creators and co-sufferers with God.

3. A further possibility is that God is best described by our human experience of relationships. More radical feminists argue for this view. The concept of God as Father is no longer acceptable because it seems to suggest a male, remote God, shaped by patriarchal culture. Instead, we need to remove all traces of patriarchy in our understanding of God. God takes on more feminine images which stress mutual relationships.

These three alternatives are not mutually exclusive. The German Lutheran theologian and pastor, Jürgen Moltmann, incorporates process and feminist elements into his traditional understanding of God. One novel feature of his writing is his re-imaging of God in social categories, but within a basically orthodox trinitarian framework. He uses the Eastern Orthodox church's idea of the co-existence of each person of the Trinity in the other and for the other and parallels this with the stress on sociality in God in feminist writing. He also allows for a participation of the world in the relationships of the Trinity. God's involvement in the world and *vice versa* is based on a loving relationship. The fundamental relationship of God with the world is that of love for the world, rather than power and dominance over the world. Moltmann believes that if we come to understand God in terms of a loving, social Trinity, this will make our attitudes to each other and creation more loving. This contrasts with an understanding of God as power over the world, which he believes is mirrored in human grasping after power over creation. His eclectic approach is welcomed by some, though he does not satisfy those feminists who argue for a replacement of traditional ideas with radical alternative concepts of God.

Moltmann shares the view of many feminist writers that we need to understand God in terms of egalitarian relationships, but go beyond this and incorporate a feminine dimension into God. Initially feminists spoke of God as Our Mother, rather than Our Father, though Moltmann prefers the idea of motherly Father. The argument against such a move is that God is beyond categories of sex, and so to describe God as female is no more or less helpful than describing God as male.

- Discuss the various options suggested by feminist writers such as God as Mother, the Holy Spirit as Female, the World as God's body. Do you think we are finding new and creative ways of thinking about God or creating God in our own image to suit our preconceived ideas?

Since the start of the feminist movement we have become much more aware of the power of language to shape attitudes. In a particular culture which has become sensitive to male words as signalling male dominance, an exclusive use of male images to describe God could give the wrong impression about God's person. We could get round this difficulty by describing God in female characteristics as Our Mother. However, this also has drawbacks as it does not satisfy those who believe that there is some significance in Christ's commandment to call God Our Father. The particular protective characteristics of God are those most characteristic of the fathers in that culture. It is doubtful if the idea of Our Mother would give a similar impression even in more liberated Western societies. Only the more extreme feminists would argue that an essential characteristic of God includes sexuality. To avoid this difficulty some theologians have opted to avoid describing God as He or She. Unfortunately, the avoidance of use of personal categories gives a clumsiness in style and tends to weaken the personal character of God.

The debate about God as Father or Mother often gives way to an understanding of the Holy Spirit in feminine categories. It seemed to solve the problem of the feminine in God in a different way as now God's 'femaleness' is concentrated in one person of the Trinity. The latter may not be a very helpful move because the Holy Spirit is traditionally the one who is immanent in the world. If the Holy Spirit is feminine, and God the Father masculine, it tends to reinforce the dichotomy between a remote, male God and an intimate, female Spirit. There is also considerable debate in Western culture as to what we mean by masculine and feminine categories. Perhaps a more fruitful approach is one which gives a feminine discussion to all the persons of the Trinity, including Christ. This is not a suggestion that we think of Jesus as androgynous, but that the qualities of both masculine and feminine are part of his person and indeed part of every person reflecting the image of Christ.

- Do you think that there are particular traits that are masculine or feminine? Do we need to reformulate our ideas about the feminine, as well as think of God in feminine categories?

The idea of describing God in motherly terms is part of the early church tradition, especially in the writings of the mystics. Hildegarde of Bingen (1098–1178) represents a Christian tradition that is fearless in affirming God's love of the earth, and thinking of the earth in maternal images as the following extracts suggest:

As the Creator loves his creation
so creation loves the Creator.
Creation, of course was fashioned to be adorned
to be showed
to be gifted with the love of the creator.
The entire world has been embraced by this kiss.

from *Meditations with Hildegarde of Bingen*,
Bear and Company 1982, p. 65

- What kind of images of God and creation does this excerpt suggest?

The Earth is at the same time mother
She is mother of all.
For contained in her
are the seeds of all.
The Earth of humankind
contains all moistness
  all verdancy
  all germinating power.
It is in so many ways fruitful.
Yet it forms not only the basic
raw material for humankind
but all the substance of God's Son.

from *Meditations with Hildegarde of Bingen,*
Bear and Company 1982, p. 51

- Do you think this quotation provides evidence of an implicit feminist theology? How would you adapt these verses to conform with contemporary feminist ideas?

The Holy Spirit is the giver of life,
The Universal Mover and root of all creation,
refiner of the world from its dross,
brings forgiveness of debts and oil for our wounds,
is radiance of life, most worthy of worship,
waking and rewaking both earth and heaven.

from Hildegarde of Bingen, *Lieder,* as cited in J. Moltmann,
The Way of Jesus Christ, SCM Press 1991, p. 251

- What does this stanza suggest about the role of the Holy Spirit in the renewal of creation?

All persons of the Trinity are in loving relationship with creation. Some feminist writers wish to go beyond this approach and suggest that the world and God are one but not identical. The world becomes God's body. God's transcendence is one which goes beyond bodily character, just as a human person is more than the material body. This attitude bears on understanding the world as a super-organism, or *Gaia*, as discussed in the chapter on Ecology and *Gaia*. While *pantheism* makes the world equivalent to God, traditional *theism* tends to make God remote from the world. *Panentheism*, on the other hand, offers a mediating position where the world is contained in God. God envelops the world, rather like the mother carrying a child in the womb. The child is both part of God, yet distinct from God. If we use this image the fundamental characteristic of God is maternal, rather than paternal.

It is possible to shift a panentheistic approach closer to a traditional view by allowing greater room for the otherness of God by a more trinitarian approach. The technical theological terms for this are the concepts of the *immanent* and *economic* Trinity. The *immanent* Trinity describes God in terms of who God is in person, as discrete from the world and as creator of the world. The *immanent* Trinity exists even before the creation of the world. Moltmann prefers to use the phrase the 'Trinity in the Origin' to describe the *immanent* Trinity. It is the opposite concept from the *immanence* of God, which describes the involvement of God in the world. The terms are confusing in that the *immanent* Trinity is God as remote from the world and as a *transcendent* Being. The *economic* Trinity, also called the *functional* Trinity, describes God as one who is active in the creation and sustaining of the world. The *economic* Trinity has nothing to do with the discipline of economics, rather it is God as actively involved and *immanent* in the world, so the *functional* Trinity is the term to be preferred. The panentheism according to a more conservative view applies to the *functional* Trinity, but not to the *immanent* Trinity.

Theologians argue about how far the functional Trinity can modify the immanent Trinity. A traditional approach keeps the essential being of the Trinity separate from the world so that the experience of the world has no effect on God. God remains discrete and all powerful. A move towards a more liberal approach allows the world to shape who God is. The experience of both suffering and creativity in the world feeds into God's experience. In this way God is One whose future is not yet certain, dependent on what happens in the world. In this case the experience of God in the world shapes the person of God. There is no sense of God's pre-existence and separate existence before the creation. Once the world becomes coterminous with God's body it becomes difficult to imagine a discrete Trinity unaffected by the world.

- Discuss whether there is a link between the way we think about God and the way we think about ourselves in relation to creation. For example, does an emphasis on mutual interrelationships in the Trinity encourage egalitarian attitudes?

- What kind of influence might emerge from a more hierarchical understanding of the Trinity with God the Father as head over the Son and Holy Spirit? Is the latter incompatible with human friendship with creation?

3. Humanity and creation as part of a community of Christ

A discussion of who Christ is comes at the interface of a discussion of God as social Trinity and humanity. The search for a deeper understanding of the person of Jesus led to the quest for the historical Jesus in liberal Protestant thought. This development in Christianity stressed the solidarity of Jesus' human nature with ours. More recently this solidarity of Jesus has come to be thought of in relation to the material, created world. Christ is incarnate as human being and is incarnate as part of material creation. Just as we come to a deeper appreciation of human beings as part of creation, so too we understand Jesus as one who shared this human material unity with creation. We are part of creation in sharing the same biology and earthly home as the rest of creation. The man Jesus, too, shares in this material unity with creation. He was dependent on the earth like any other human being.

The link between Jesus Christ and creation is not just with reference to his human nature, in solidarity with us as part of creation. Jesus as Christ is the cosmic Lord who offers the hope of the resurrection to all of creation, not just to human beings. The biblical basis of such a move comes from reflection on passages such as Col. 1.1–15 and Rom. 8.18–25. There is some academic debate about how Christ and creation are related. Some argue that Christ comes to save creation directly. Others suggest that salvation for creation is mediated via the healing effect of Christ on human relationships with creation. The first alternative is the more radical view since it seems to suggest that Christ's action was directed to creation in itself as well as that damage to creation effected through human sinfulness. Both alternatives lead to the conclusion that the significance of Christ is cosmic, rather than narrowly concerned for human interests alone. (For a discussion of Bible passages see chapter 2 on Ecology and Biblical Studies.)

The task of humanity is to become the image of Christ. Christ is the *perfect* image of God spoken about in Gen. 1.27 when human beings are described as those who are made in the image of God. Jesus Christ is one who exists in relationship with the two other persons of the Trinity. We could take the next step and say that Christ is defined by these relationships. Just as Christ in the Holy Trinity exists in fellowship and friendship, so too humanity should strive to exist in an interdependent community which includes creation. Our ability to become the perfect image of God and Christ-like is reflected in our ability to coexist in relationships with others and with creation. In this sense we participate in the life of the Trinity and become not just the image of God, but the image of God as defined in terms of the image of the Trinity. The coming of the Holy Spirit to the human Christian community is a visble sign that the reconciliation between human beings and God, and human beings and creation has begun already. It is the beginning of humanity becoming the image of the Trinity.

- Discuss whether you think there are any distinctions between God's relation to human beings and God's relation to non-human creation? In what way does God as Trinity come into your discussion?

- What are the ways in which Christ can be a model for human relationships to each other and creation?

In the past some scholars believe that we have permitted an interpretation of the command to have dominion over all creation in Gen. 1.28 as a licence to dominate creation and treat it as a resource for human benefit. A movement away from this approach is one which insists that the concept of dominion in Genesis means stewardship rather than domination. However, stewardship still allows us to treat nature in a way which keeps humanity fully in control: we are managing the planet, even if in a benign rather than malicious way. (For a further discussion on this see chapter 2.)

Those feminist theologians who draw on scripture believe that the fault in our interpretation of Genesis has been a failure to recognize the ideal of co-operation between men and women in the care of creation. The ideas of exploitation, then, emerged because there was an over-emphasis on male control, first over women and second over the earth. They reinterpret early chapters of Genesis which seem to suggest a domination of women by men. Gen. 2.7, for example, suggests that males were formed first and Gen. 2.15 that men were given the task of management of the earth. The creation of women from the rib of Adam seems to imply a superiority of men, women being created as a helper in the male task of responsibility over creation. The Fall can also be interpreted in a way which portrays women in a negative light. The fault is traced to the folly of Eve who tempts Adam against his better judgment. The command of God that man should rule over women in Gen. 3.16 is a fitting outcome given the folly of Adam in listening to Eve before the Fall. A reinterpretation of the text along feminist lines could be as follows. Adam before the creation of Eve stands, not as the first male, but as the androgynous figure who represents the origin of humanity. The idea of human beings bearing the image of God in Gen. 1.26 is followed in the biblical text by the affirmation of human beings as male and female in Gen. 1.27. Feminist theologians believe that the sequence here is significant and that our image bearing *depends* on our cooperation as male and female. The Fall is the equal responsibility of Adam and Eve. The charge to Eve that she will be ruled by her husband in Gen. 3.16 and the charge to Adam that he will plough the earth happens after the Fall. A return to the more ideal state in Gen. 1.27 is a return to more egalitarian responsibility. Further, unless we replace our understanding of the human community with more egalitarian perspectives, we cannot hope to change our attitude to creation as a whole.

A feminist approach puts emphasis on a more *holistic* attitude to existence. The spiritual and material are not separate, but bound up with each other. They argue that the high status given to rationality and spirit promoted a negative attitude towards women, who in the past were considered to be less rational than men and of lower status. It seems to me that the link between material and spiritual is also a practical outcome of a *return* to the cosmic way of perceiving the world that is characteristic of Eastern Orthodoxy and Celtic Christianity. It is of interest that Celtic culture was much more affirming towards women and also had a deep respect for nature. However, their understanding of God was fully orthodox and Trinitarian. In other words, a sense of understanding ourselves in communion with creation does not necessarily force us to re-image Christ and God in radical ways. In both instances the possibility of human friendship with creation emerges. Above all the value of creation comes from perceiving it as a gift and as beloved of God and in communion with Christ. The separation between the material world and the spiritual is replaced by a deeper awareness of the sacramental presence of God as Holy Spirit in all creation. The more orthodox understanding is that the creation shows us the light of the Creator, but creation still remains clearly distinct from the Creator. In this case all of creation participates in the love of God. The more radical understanding is that the creation is itself a part of God so that to try and make any distinctions is not helpful (See the discussion in chapter 3 on Ecology and Celtic Christianity and the practical implications in chapter 5 on Ecology and Ethics.)

- The *Shalom* or peaceful coexistence between God, humanity and nature is a vision for the future. Are there practical ways in which this vision can begin to become a reality in your present context?

5

Ecology and Ethics

1. Specific problems of environmental ethics

Ethics, by definition, seeks to discover principles which underlie human action. The specific task of *environmental ethics* is to develop principles regarding human action in the non-human world. It has, then, a practical goal in view and so is not just a description of the place of humans in the universe or a justification of an ethical system between humans. It is the practical issues, too, which impinge on the study of ethics. The size, urgency and complexity of environmental issues is reflected in the size, urgency and complexity of associated ethical questions.

Example

Consider the following hypothetical situation. A farmer in the UK decides to increase the yield of his wheat crop by giving a high dosage of nitrogen fertilizers. This, in turn, leads to a greater multiplication of pests which attack this crop. The wheat is more vulnerable to disease as it is genetically uniform. This is the consequence of artificial breeding to produce high-yield varieties which take out the natural variability within a wild strain. If he tried to grow a wild strain the yields would be much poorer, but it would be less subject to disease. He decides to spray the crop with pesticides in order to keep the yields high. The market pressure to produce cheap wheat is high since there are other competing sources from Canada and the USA. The public demand for cheaper food keeps the prices down with a low profit margin. Unfortunately, the high level of nitrates originating from the fertilizers runs into the river water nearby and means that it is no longer acceptable for human consumption. Also the pesticides have killed a large number of fish so that local fishermen go out of business.

- Which has priority, the business practice of the farmer, who like everyone else, has to make a living wage, or restraint on ecological damage?

- Is the farmer responsible directly for putting the livelihood of fishermen at risk, as well as the health of the local population? Who should pay compensation? Should we blame the seed producers who supply monocultures that are susceptible to pesticides? Or should we blame the researchers who produce the seed? Or the market forces of society for demanding cheap food? Or the government for not giving subsidies in the event of possible crop failure?

- Which takes priority, the short-term interest of the farmer and the need for food in the population, or the long-term interest of the ecosystem and the possible long-term damage to the health of the population?

- Should we take into account the damaging effect on wildlife that has no apparent influence on the human community? In other words, is it unethical to damage non-human species, regardless of whether this affects our own immediate interests?

- How far should we take into account the loss of wilderness as a place for human recreation and aesthetic interest? If all the available land is cultivated, it becomes a very bland landscape. How do we measure such values?

- How far should such considerations affect the actions of farmers in the poorer countries of the Southern hemisphere?

The above example shows how one relatively simple action by a farmer can have all kinds of ethical ramifications in areas outside his immediate farming interest. In those countries of the world where farming is practised for the immediate survival interests of the family the problems become more acute. In the above case a UK farmer might be able to choose to supplement his income by other means, for example through setting up a small business. The wherewithal and expertise to make such choices are not always possible in poorer communities. We hinted at the effect of world trade on the price of goods. This brings us into the area of Ecology and Politics which we will discuss in more detail in chapter 8.

The above example also shows how we need a way of discerning fundamental ethical principles on which to act in given situations. The fierce debate in environmental ethics is how to define and implement such principles. In the sections which follow I will show how there is ambiguity and debate in the definition of the ethical basis for environmental action. Some of the theoretical ethical positions are less workable than others in terms of helping us to understand what kind of action we can take in given situations. I will, therefore, give concrete examples as test cases in order to clarify how each principle will work in given practical situations.

2. What is the value of 'nature?'

I am using 'nature' in the present context to describe non-human creation. It is necessary to define the term 'nature' as it lends itself to ambiguity for the following reasons. Human beings are part of 'nature' in that we share in the biochemical and physiological processes in common with animals and all living beings. We are also 'apart' from nature in that we are self-aware and have the power to make conscious decisions about how to change the natural world around us. The debate in environmental ethics is how we, as human beings, should give value to the natural world. If we regard nature as a resource to be managed for human interests, it has *instrumental* value. If we regard nature as having value in and of itself it has *inherent* value. This is often used by ethicists to refer to the value of something, with the assumption that a valuing *subject* is present. For example, a wood has inherent value to the owner as long as s/he is present. If we regard nature as having *intrinsic* value, this is independent of humans, or their presence as a valuing subject.

Example

Consider the following example taken from biotechnology. It was envisaged in the late 1980s, but as far as I am aware has not succeeded in reaching the field experimental stage. The aim was to introduce the genetic material for nitrogen fixation from leguminous plants such as peas, clover and so on into cereal wheat crop plants.

Nitrogen fixation is the technical term which biologists use to describe the way free nitrogen is turned into a form which is accessible for plant nutrition. Plants are remarkable compared with animals in their ability to turn inorganic nitrogen compounds, such as ammonia and nitrate, into amino acids and proteins. This makes them *primary* producers of protein from inorganic sources. The leguminous plants rely on associated bacteria living in special parts of the roots of the plant known as nodules in order to fix free nitrogen. The plant and bacteria are dependent on each other for *mutual benefit* in a *symbiotic* relationship. Such fixation of nitrogen by the bacteria also benefits the *host* plant and reduces the need for high doses of fertilizer, in the form of nitrate or ammonium, though these plants can use these sources of nitrogen as well.

The wheat/bacteria symbiosis project, if successful, could have enormous impact on the requirement for fertilizers and so the modified wheat plant would be patented. However, from a scientific point of view, there are considerable difficulties in transferring all the genes which allow the legumes to form a symbiotic relationship with the bacteria to the recipient wheat plants. In order to create a new symbiosis between wheat and bacteria we may need to alter the genetic material in the bacteria as well. If we make such an alteration we risk releasing into the environment a modified microbe, which could have far reaching effects in field conditions. It is not easy to predict what these effects might be. What are the alternative ethical responses?

1. From an *instrumental* stance we could argue that the difficulty of making this particular project work in field trials

means that the project has theoretical rather than practical interest. It should not, therefore, be funded by companies interested in introducing new crops for farmers. On the other hand the potential for human benefit may make it worth our while taking the risk of involvement in this particular project.

2. From the stance of *inherent* worth we could argue that as subjects we have become potential creators of a new form of wheat that has value to ourselves in relation to human achievement. The technical skill involved in making these manipulations is the marvel of the latest insights in human co-operation with nature. Here we assume that there are limits to our action that are part of the system itself. In other words, the natural wheat plant would not be able to receive genetic material that is in some way 'dangerous' to its life, or if it did these plants would die in the selection process.

3. From the point of view of *intrinsic* worth we could argue that these modifications are not giving due respect to the value of nature in and of itself. The so-called choice implied by the second position, above, is not a real one as far as the plants or bacteria are concerned. An added anxiety is that if we have the technology for manipulation at this level for crop plants, it could be used in trans-specific experiments in higher animals or between humans and chimpanzees, for example. Are we not attempting to 'play God' and so step outside our limits?

- Set up a role play between those who argue for instrumental, inherent or intrinsic value of nature.

Environmental ethicists often talk about the need to give nature 'intrinsic' worth, but do not think through what this might mean for environmentally directed research, such as in the example given above. The 'intrinsic' worth of nature has been defined by some ethicists as that which allows the 'interests' of the organism concerned to be realized. These interests are *basic*, if they are fundamental to the survival of the organism, or *peripheral* if they are not fundamental. The above example shows how money and resources could be given to a project which cannot be said in the short term to be for the basic interest of either the plants or humans. We are left with the dilemma: does the *potential* to meet the basic interest of humans outweigh the violation to the basic interest of the plants?

- Discuss where we should put limits on biotechnology practice in animal, plant and human genetic manipulation. How should these limits be enforced?

3. The basis for environmental ethics: is it centred around human concern or non-human nature?

A more traditional ethical approach assumes that our values depend on what is best for the individuals and groups within the *human* community. The starting point for ethical discussion is what is best for human interest and is termed *anthropocentric*. This view is being challenged by those who wish to extend the value given to human beings to include animals and/or plants. The position in this case is known as *biocentric*. Those who campaigned for the adoption of *animal rights* presupposed a move away from anthropocentrism towards biocentrisim.

If we chose to develop a specially Christian approach to environmental ethics, there are arguments both for and against taking an anthropocentric stance. Those who believe that Christianity is anthropocentric argue along the following lines:

1. The idea of humankind made in the image of God puts human beings in a unique relationship with God compared with other creatures. Our unique relationship gives us a special *responsibility* to act as stewards or caretakers of creation.

2. This caretaking role is clear from the passages in Genesis where God commands human beings to have dominion over creation and subdue the earth. This is a mandate for care of the earth, rather than its exploitation. If we fail to nurture the earth we fail in responsibility as stewards of creation. Our special human privileges or 'rights' go hand in hand with special human 'duties'. It therefore does not make much sense to speak about the 'rights' of nature or those of animals, since they are not in a position to take responsibility.

On the other hand there are equally convincing arguments which suggest a Christian approach to environmental ethics needs to be biocentric:

1. All of creation shares to some extent in the image of God, not just human beings. God loves creation for itself in a way that is not dependent on whether creation is directed towards human benefit. A proper attitude towards creation is one which is cosmic in approach, rather than narrowly directed towards human interest. The 'rights' of nature are linked to its worth to God and do not need to be directly linked to 'responsibilities'. A Christian approach is to give rights to those who are pushed to the margins and who, for medical or other reasons, are restricted in their ability to assume responsibility.

2. The practical issues of the environmental crisis show that an anthropocentric attitude is unhelpful and potentially damaging. The command to 'have dominion' has too often been interpreted as a licence for 'domination'. In this way an anthropocentric Christian approach is partly to blame for the crisis.

- Set up a debate between those who argue from an anthropocentric or biocentric position, arguing from a Christian perspective. Which argument do you find the most convincing?

- The biocentric view leads to the development of pressure groups concerned for animal rights. There are specific organizations which campaign against the use of animals in science, and for the dissolution of commercial agriculture and the elimination of commercial and sport hunting and trapping. Discuss the ethical arguments for and against such practices.

Case study: the Brazilian forests

Consider the following example as a way of clarifying the practical outcome of a biocentric or anthropocentric view. The direct causes of rain forest depletion are agriculture, logging for timber and industry, cattle ranching and 'development'. There are other causes such as human population growth, the survival needs of the poor and world demand for forest products. The world demand for timber leaves behind a trail of wastage and ecological destruction. On the other hand the sale of these goods is essential to meet the need for foreign currency in order to pay back loans from the earlier 'development' programme. In this situation it is far from clear who takes responsibility and whose interests have priority. The possible different approaches we could adopt are:

1. On the basis of an *anthropocentric* view we could argue that the survival needs of the Brazilian people outweigh the damage to the ecosystem. On the other hand there is room for debate here, since we could argue that in the long term human survival is threatened both directly by the removal of the timber resource and indirectly by changing the climate through an increase in carbon dioxide level in the atmosphere. (For a development of this debate see section 4 of this chapter, and also chapter 1 on Practical Issues of Environmental Concern.)

2. On the basis of a *biocentric* view we could argue that the tropical rain forest should be left for the sake of the non-human species which are confined to this ecosystem. We could add to this the question of human interest by including the potential value for medicine and other uses of the forest plants which have not yet been identified.

Whether we adopt the biocentric or anthropocentric view we have the added complication of deciding who has the priority interest within the human community. The 'blame' for the destruction of the rainforest can be narrowly directed against the poor of the land, or against the multinational companies, government officials or world economic system. The underlying driving force towards the destruction is not easy to decipher in these circumstances.

• Set up a debate between those acting on behalf of indigenous people, timber agencies, government officials, environmental pressure groups. Decide whether each group would take up an anthropocentric or biocentric view.

The above example also illustrates the close entanglement of ethical issues concerned with justice and 'integrity' of creation. Another theme, that of peace, would apply if there was fighting over scarce resources or if some of the money gained from timber logging was used for military purposes, as is often the case in politically unstable parts of the Two-Thirds World. The World Council of Churches (WCC) was among those who recognized how these factors have an important bearing on each other. WCC set up a number of consultations to discuss these issues. The general work of the WCC first began to expand in this field with the Vancouver Assembly in 1983. The theme that emerged from this assembly was 'Justice, Peace and the Integrity of Creation' or JPIC. The assembly recognized that environmental problems need to be tackled alongside questions to do with justice issues such as human rights and alongside questions to do with peace such as nuclear disarmament. The ethical issues involved in all three areas of justice, peace and environment are closely inter-twined.

- Discuss the possible links between justice towards each other and justice to the earth. How does the issue of peace apply to the earth?

The term 'integrity of creation' coined at the WCC assembly is a way of reinforcing the belief that human beings are part of the totality of creation. It is also a shorthand way of describing the dependence of creation in relation to the Creator and the intrinsic value of creation. It could be used to support a more 'biocentric' view compared with a more 'anthropocentric' position. The *liberation* of human beings from oppressive structures could then become extended to include the liberation of nature from human manipulation.

- What does the liberation of nature imply in practice? Would scientific research still be feasible?

- Discuss practical ways in which justice, peace and the integrity of creation can become an integral part of church life. For example, draw up a covenant between a church in the Fens in the UK and one overseas in an area such as Bangladesh where there is extensive deforestation and flooding. Both parts of the world are vulnerable to a rise in sea level caused by global warming. The latter comes from the burning of fossil fuels and destruction of the rainforest (see chapter 1). This covenant could be an agreement to reduce greenhouse gases, in the Fens by a reduction in burning fossil fuels and in Bangladesh by forest replantation.

The shift which took place at the Vancouver Assembly was from a pragmatic instrumental attitude: that is the earth is to be managed wisely for human benefit, to one which respected the intrinsic value of creation. Consultations took place in Africa (Nairobi 1981), Latin America (Buenos Aires 1985) and South East Asia (Manila 1986). In all three consultations the local groups reported the close association of justice, peace and environmental issues. The European Assembly in Basle, Switzerland, in 1989 included Roman Catholics as well as delegates from the Orthodox, Anglican and Protestant churches. The Roman Catholics in previous meetings participated as observers, rather than as full delegates. The conference made a number of specific recommendations for justice, such as ethical investment and regulation of international trade. They also recommended continued disarmament negotiations, a ban on testing nuclear weapons and outlawing of weapons of mass destruction. Their environmental policy included the reduction of energy use, the development of renewable energy supplies, measures to protect the ozone layer and the recognition of the need for international law on species preservation, waste disposal and genetic engineering.

The ethical perspective that emerged from these ecumenical consultations was one which encouraged a God-centred or *theocentric* view, which holds together human interest and the broader concern for the natural world. In a sense it is beyond either an anthropocentric or biocentric approach. It recognizes the value of all creation, but also sees the place of human responsibility. If we take a theocentric view as a basis for ethics then our understanding of God shapes the way we behave in a closer way than if we remain anthropocentric or biocentric. For example, if we believe that God is radically separate from the world then our behaviour will have little effect on God. It becomes easier to adopt an ethic suited to human interest alone.

On the other hand, if we believe that God is fundamentally involved in the world, then our behaviour will affect God and we are more likely to adopt an ethic that takes into account the interests of non-humans. Further, if we believe that the fundamental characteristic of God is that of loving Creator, rather than Power over the Universe, then God's love extends to the whole of creation in its complexity, not just individual species. I will draw out the practical dilemmas facing ethicists in this respect in the section which follows. See also chapter 4 on Ecology, Women and Christian Community for a description of different models of God.

- Does a theocentric ethic avoid the problems associated with a biocentric or anthropocentric position, but create new difficulties?

4. Should primary ethical concern be for individuals or groups and systems?

Ethics has always had two areas for discussion:

1. Broader concerns about the *ethos* or cultural milieu in which we find ourselves.

2. Specific problems such as the conservation or preservation of species.

The debate in environmental ethics about the priority of individuals or groups falls into the second category (2), though the answers to these questions also bear on the first category (1). In order to clarify the debate, consider the example of the farmer using fertilizers and pesticides on his wheat fields. In this instance the damage is done to the whole ecosystem, not just a particular species. The extent of the damage will depend partly on the selectivity of the herbicides and pesticides. Here we have an instance of damage to individual plants and organisms, as well as damage to the *system as a whole*. The ethical debate would need to consider the *value* of this whole, also known as *systemic* value, in addition to the value of particular species. For example, some rare plants may be growing at a nearby site, and if these were killed the damage would include the value of this species.

- Do you think that subjectivity is unavoidable if we decide to protect some species rather than others?

The ethical dilemma is taking account of these different values and making the best possible decision. Such decisions always involve an element of *risk* caused partly by our own ignorance and partly by a lack of secure knowledge of the future. For example, we might let the farmer carry on his farming practice with limited use of fertilizer and pesticides, but we may not have sufficient data on the long term use of such chemicals. The risk of potential damage to the ecosystem may be outweighed by the interests of the individual farmer.

- What ethical principles could we use to help us make a decision about fertilizer and pesticide use by farmers? Are the risks ever eliminated? If not how do we build in controls on acceptable risks?

- Refer back to the example given on biotechnology in the section on the value of nature. Do you think there are ways of building in acceptable risks? Are constraints on genetic engineering sufficient or are we unwise to attempt any such trans-specific manipulations?

In the hypothetical example given above of the farmer using fertilizers and pesticides on his wheat fields, we could also ask ourselves: What happens if a particular species that was near to extinction was threatened by pesticide application, but this species was *not* an essential part of the ecosystem? For example, one of Britain's most threatened plants is a variety of whitebeam known as *Sorbus leyana*. This plant does not seem to have any particular 'usefulness' to human welfare, nor is it an essential component in an ecosystem. In this case the species could be said to have high individual value, but have little *systemic* value, i.e. value to the system as a whole. A related debate is whether we value individual plants within a species, or can give value to the species as a whole. If whales and pandas were not near to extinction as a species we might not be so concerned about the threat to individual mammals. Some ethicists argue that the value of the species is not different from the value given to individuals within that species. Both have intrinsic or inherent value.

- Discuss how we could distinguish between essential and non-essential species. Is their importance related to (a) their value to humans, (b) their value to the ecosystem or (c) their value in themselves. How might an atheist support (c)?

- Do you think the value of individuals is the same as the value given to the species as a whole?

Whatever scheme we adopt it is often necessary to make hard choices between working for the protection of one species rather than another. In practice those species which are most threatened are given the most protection. The scale of value is also influenced by the complexity of the species concerned. Those species which are more advanced on the evolutionary tree tend to have priority over the humbler lower organisms such as protozoa and insects. In other words even if we adopt a 'biocentric' view, in practice we still have to make choices between saving individual organisms over others. These choices require us to take *risks* in that we do not know what the *ultimate* outcome of such choices will be. What happens if we decide to protect a higher animal when other organisms which are not protected are more crucial to the overall ecosystem? The introduction of the idea of *systemic* value is an important check on such choices, but the risk factor is never eliminated.

The risk factors are also part of the discussion of environmental issues operative at a global level. The greenhouse effect, for example, raises some fundamental ethical issues. (For a discussion of the greenhouse effect, see the section on climatic change in chapter 1 on Practical Issues of Environmental Concern.) While there is a broad consensus that there is a rise in temperature associated with the rise in carbon dioxide levels, not all scientists are convinced that there is a direct link between climatic change and carbon dioxide levels. There are other factors which could come into effect to change weather conditions such as the presence of pollutant and dust particles which screen out the sun's rays.

- Given this uncertainty, discuss the risks inherent in the following alternatives:
  (i) Assume that global climatic warming *is* correlated with carbon dioxide levels and act on behalf of the whole global system and work for the reduction of greenhouses gases regardless of cost to individual nations.
  (ii) Assume that these predictions are not watertight in which case we take into account social factors such as the livelihood of individual groups such as the coal miners.

5. The debate over 'deep' and 'shallow' ecology

This debate bears on the issue I have just discussed in 4, above. Those who argue for the 'deep' ecology position insist that the value of the whole is ultimately of more significance than the individual parts. In practice this is a way of moving from anthropocentrism to *holism*. This is subtly different from biocentrism. In the biocentric view, which we discussed under 3 above, the value given to humans is *extended* to include all living creatures. For holism and deep ecology the interconnectedness between everything is essential, so that we arrive at a *new basis* on which to define value. It is not simply an extension of human values, but a new axiom.

We might ask ourselves how humans or even God fits into this new way of viewing nature. Here we arrive at some of the difficulties with this view. Humanity appears to come to a self-realization through identification with the natural world. We become merged into the world in a way which has mystical overtones.

For 'deep' ecologists, those who choose to value nature according to human interests alone or as of primary concern are given the pejorative label of 'shallow' ecologists. The concern for the environment is there, but it is based on human interest. This is not adequate as far as deep ecologists are concerned. For them there can be no real change in our relationship with nature until we shift our understanding of how humans and nature are interconnected.

- Is it possible to be both a Christian and a 'deep' ecologist? or a Christian and a 'shallow' ecologist? Discuss ways in which theological principles might modify either a 'shallow' or a 'deep' approach.

A Creation-centred spirituality is cosmic . . . The more and more deeply one sinks into our cosmic existence the more fully one realizes the truth that there does not exist an inside and an outside cosmos, but rather one cosmos; we are in the cosmos and the cosmos is in us . . . All things are inter-related because all things are microcosms of a macrocosm. And it is all in motion, it is all en route, it is all moving, vibrant, dancing and full of surprises. It is all a blessing, an ongoing and fertile blessing with a holy, salvic history of about twenty billion years.

Matthew Fox, *Original Blessing*, Bear 1983, p. 69

- What are the theological and practical consequences of adopting creation-centred spirituality, such as that outlined above? Debate the theological presuppositions of this view.

6

Ecology and Liturgy

1. Liturgy shaping our thought and action

In our contemporary context there is a growing sympathy towards creating liturgies which will embody a sense of concern for environmental issues. However, alongside this openness to creation of new liturgies there is a fear of New Age, paganism, syncretism and 'nature' religion. Part of this fear is the anxiety that Christian truth is somehow corrupted by including creation themes. This is especially true where creation themes seem to imply a form of identity between God and creation or *pantheism*. Historically, Christianity has taken over the festivals and places of worship of pagan, earth-centred 'folk' religion, so that an inclusion of more earthly themes could trigger a fear of a return to paganism. In this chapter I will explore some of the ways in which we can begin to create liturgies which do celebrate creation in a Christian way without giving way to either a fear of past heresies or a loss in affinity with fundamental Christian truths.

The way liturgy works in the life of a community is much more powerful than the simple content of doctrine. For the majority of churchgoers the experience of participating in the liturgy is the only regular place where they will receive explicit Christian 'formation'. The liturgy allows an openness to God in a way that includes but transcends the teaching of biblical truth, doctrine and reflection found in the sermon or homily. It is possible that during liturgical acts we are in a particular mode of thinking which makes us more receptive and less analytical. The point I am making here is that liturgy 'forms' people in both explicit and implicit ways which in many respects have a more powerful influence than explicit teaching.

Liturgy and life are closely related in Christian orthodoxy, so that liturgy becomes part of Christian living. The liturgy of the Western church has tended to stress the mortification of the flesh and human sinfulness, while the liturgy of the Eastern church has put greater emphasis on the celebratory aspects coming from the resurrection. At the centre of worship in the church we discover the eucharist, which also expresses the transformation of creation through God the Holy Spirit. The eucharist reminds us of both the passion and resurrection of Christ. The ecological crisis calls for a greater awareness of a failure to recognize human responsibility to care for creation, as well as a celebration of the gift of life. It calls for a new beginning, an attitude of repentance, or more broadly a *metanoia*. The fundamental change in attitude becomes possible through a deeper participation in the liturgical life of the church.

- What has been your experience of liturgy from childhood to the present day? Make a memory journey and chart those periods where your experience changed. Exchange ideas in group discussions about how your particular experiences fitted in with a particular stage of your personal development.

2. What are the building blocks of liturgy?

The following components form the basis of established liturgies:

(a) Explicit Christian assertions

The best known summaries of explicit assertions are the creeds. 'I believe in God: *Creator* of heaven and earth.' The traditional creeds have a widely accepted authority in established churches. Other statements within the liturgy are also explicit in terms of their witness to Christian faith in a Creator, but carry less authority in the church. For example, certain prayers, such as the blessing prayers used in the Catholic eucharistic liturgy as well as

certain hymns and songs, make the Christian message explicit.
It is interesting that they are similar to the blessing prayers of
the Jewish tradition. 'Blessed be God, Lord of all creation.
Through your goodness we have this wine to offer, fruit of the
vine and work of human hands. It will become our spiritual
drink.'

Biblical passages allow for more direct teaching of the basic
tenets of Christian faith, though the exposition of these is
confined to the homily or sermon. Those taking part in the
liturgy often find that more explicit teaching comes through
instruction *outside* the context of the liturgy. In a sense the
liturgy is an affirmation of the beliefs of the community,
though participants are bound to appropriate its *theological*
content at different levels. While there are explicit references to
Christian belief, the theological content is normally *presupposed* and implicit, as we will explore further below. At one
level some in the community will accept the truth of these
statements without question. At another level some will question the assumptions, meaning and purpose of these statements
in order to arrive at a deeper understanding of the theology of
the church. At a further level some will question the interpretation given by the church and will seek to arrive at their own
conclusions.

In what liturgies are there *explicit* references to the themes of
creation? It strikes me that there are two possible sources where
the idea of creation is spelt out and affirmed. One possible source
is the traditional liturgy found in the Orthodox church, which has
remained largely unchanged through the centuries and is particularly rich in its celebration of creation and acknowledgment of
the love of God for all the earth. In the words of one Orthodox
theologian:

> *Every day* in our Vespers we sing Psalm 103 which says: 'Bless
> the Lord all his works. In all places of his dominion, bless the
> Lord O my soul.'[1]

The continual reference to creation themes contrasts with the
relative lack of reference to creation in other liturgies.

- Examine a liturgy used by your own church community. How many references to creation themes can you find? Discuss whether you think this is adequate and how you might be able to introduce changes. Do you think you have the authority to make changes in the liturgy?

A second possible source is *contemporary* creation liturgies. The *Creation Harvest Liturgy*, published by WWF/ICOREC in 1987, is explicit in its affirmation of the Christian belief in creation. A section from it appears in Appendix 1. There are other unofficial sources of liturgies which affirm creation written from the context of women's experience, such as those written by the St Hilda Community.[2] Other examples are in the liturgies created by the Iona Community, three of which also appear in Appendix 1.

(b) Indirect theological assertions

The most obvious place where theology becomes implicit is in the hymnology and prayers. An analysis of the hymns we sing shows that many traditional ones are focussed on guilt and sin and a rejection or contempt for material earthly realities. The following verses were written by Bianco da Siena in the fifteenth century and translated by R. F. Littledale in the nineteenth century. They appear in, for example, *Hymns Ancient and Modern*:

> Come down, O Love divine,
> seek thou this soul of mine,
> and visit it with thine own ardour glowing;
> O Comforter draw near,
> within my heart appear,
> and kindle it, thy holy flame bestowing.
>
> O let it freely burn,
> till earthly passions turn
> to dust and ashes in its heat consuming;
> and let thy glorious light
> shine ever on my sight,
> and clothe me round, the while my path illuming.

We are encouraged to allow 'earthly passions' to turn to 'dust and ashes' in the fire of God's love. This is just one example among many. As we express contempt for material things it encourages a devaluation of the natural world. It could eventually lead to a hardening of attitudes towards environmental problems.

- Use your hymn book to find hymns which seem to express contempt for material things. When you have found implicit themes make these explicit by drawing up a list of those assumptions or *presuppositions* of the hymn writer which you can glean from the hymn. Can you find any similar themes in the New Testament?

(c) Metaphors and symbols

Metaphors and symbols are created through the liturgy in a way which builds up our perception of God, the world and our inter-relationships. The exploration of the way metaphors function to shape our understanding is a vast area that is out of the scope of this chapter. Briefly, I am using the term metaphorical thinking to describe the way we can spot a *thread* of similarity between two *dissimilar* objects or events. Thinking symbolically, on the other hand, expresses the similarity between objects or events. Both metaphors and symbols work to create *images*. Sallie McFague suggests that the Protestant tradition is more at home with metaphors, which sees dissimilarity and contrast between God and creation, while the Catholic sensibility works with symbols and sees similarity, connection and harmony between God and creation.[3]

Feminist writers are especially sensitive to the issue of images since many of the key metaphors for God or Christ such as Father, Judge and King could encourage a lack of human responsibility and passivity. The metaphor for nature as female in the writings of the first natural scientists seems to encourage an exploitation of the natural world alongside the suppression of women (see also chapter 4 on Ecology, Women and Christian Community). Consider the following graphic imagery of God as midwife, based on a reflection on Psalm 22.9–10.

God our midwife . . .
Contain in your hands
the breaking of waters,
the blood and din of your birth:
then, through our tears and joy, deliverer,
your wrinkled, infant kingdom may be born.
Amen

Gill Paterson, Christian Aid

• Study a traditional prayer book and find the metaphors which are used for God. Compare this with the above prayer. What kind of relationship between God and humanity would be encouraged by each image?

The cross represents a shared image most widely used throughout the Christian churches.

• Do the two different traditions of leaving Christ on the cross in the Catholic tradition and an empty cross in the Protestant tradition tell you anything about whether the cross is functioning as a symbol or metaphor in each case? Which image do you find the most powerful and why?

There are imaginative ways to include the sense that Christ's suffering and our suffering is linked with the suffering of creation. Traditionally we have used fresh green leaves etc. as imagery to express the themes of resurrection and new life. However, we could equally express the suffering of creation through interweaving plants in association with the cross.

(d) Non-verbal actions and gestures

Another major question which surfaces in the creation of liturgy is the use of non-verbal actions and gestures. Care and attention to these aspects are part of liturgical practice especially in those churches which hold to a sacramental view of creation. I am dealing here with those aspects of the liturgy which encourage a movement (or lack of movement) by the worshippers, the location of symbols and images and people in the church building, sounds, visual images and handling or tasting of material elements. In the Othordox church, for example, the blessing of the water affirms the blessing of creation. For:

> The blessing of the waters shows us the sanctifying and redemptive power given to an element of creation through the invocation of the Holy Spirit by the church. The blessings for all manner of natural elements such as the fields, vineyards and first fruits, wheat, etc., show how the Church recognizes the transformation of all aspects of creation through the salvation and glorification of humanity and thus of all creation.[4]

There are other examples of gestures which have indirect theological associations in the Catholic church. Practices, such as the use of incense, holy water, genuflecting, lighting candles, crossing oneself are commonplace in the Catholic tradition. The Protestant tradition in its more Calvinist mode rejects such practices. Such lack of action could reinforce a belief that matter is separate from spirit. The misuse of symbols and images which can come through a confusion of the symbol with the reality it expresses may be behind the concern to abstain from all such practices. Other dangers emerge if the participants in the liturgy believe that attention to the details of symbolism is a prerequisite for adoration of God. The symbols and images are present as guides, to remind us of the involvement of God in creation.

- Make a list of all the non-verbal aspects which are part of your church tradition. What does each action or symbol add to the liturgy?

- Set up a debate between those in favour of extensive use of symbolism, such as candles, incense, bells etc. and those against. What are the historical roots of the conflict?

(e) Liturgical action

The language we can use to describe this concept is rather elusive. I am referring here to the hidden dynamic in the liturgical act as a whole which incorporates physical movement and procession, but goes much deeper than this in terms of what is happening during the entire rite. It expresses the flow of action in the course of the liturgy. We can assess the 'shape' of the liturgy by reading through the whole rite and asking questions such as:

How far are the themes directed to promote interests of the individual or the community?

- Read one of the liturgies that has been in use in your church for some years. Try to think of all the areas which are not covered by the liturgy. What conclusions do you draw from this exercise?

Does the flow of the liturgy encourage an inward-looking or outward-looking attitude?

- Discuss the value of processions/corporate acts at different places in the liturgy, for example the particular practice adopted for the movement to receive communion in a eucharistic liturgy.

Is the liturgy always centred on faith in God and Jesus Christ, or are some other themes threatening to become more important?

- What themes have you noticed in your church? Is this possibility relevant?

We can sometimes weaken the impact of a liturgy directed outwards to the wider community by the way we phrase prayers. Political issues, for example, are often prayed about in a way which is deliberately perceived as not taking sides. For example, we might pray in a general way for 'the situation' in a particular place where there is conflict, even when there is an obvious aggressor. This can make the impact of such prayers seem diffuse. Alternatively, we might avoid the political questions altogether. If the intercessions and confessions are confined to individual needs and individual sins the flow of the liturgy tends to be directed towards the individual. A focus on individual sin avoids the challenge to social structures and global injustices. If we confine political issues to special services to mark particular events, this is another way of avoiding the challenge to make weekly liturgy concerned with public issues as well as private faith. The implication is that we are deemed to be powerless to effect change. Thus events are left unmentioned and by implication seem to be either unimportant or heretical.

3. A practical approach to writing ecological liturgies

(a) Guidelines for liturgical writing

The way liturgy can, in practice, come to exist in a way that is meaningful and helpful takes account of the following:

1. It is well integrated with the central themes of Christian faith. The *seasonal* themes of the church's year such as Advent, Christmas, Lent, Easter and Pentecost could allow the drama of salvation to become echoed in ecological language. The following prayer is part of the Liturgy for Advent. It could also be used during Lent. For an example of an extract from a Harvest Liturgy, see Appendix 1.

> We, your people, come.
> We who crucify this world,
> stripping bare its soil,
> crowning it with a wreath of broken trees.
> Its air breathes painfully,
> its waters weep for the folly that poisons them,
> its creatures bleed.
> We have eaten and drunk of life's body.
>
> Heirs of all,
> we have sold our world.
> Thirty pieces of silver is our price.
> Loudly declaring our love,
> We have denied our Lord.
>
> We are Judas,
> We are Peter.
> We are the cross of all creation.
>
> Lord, in your advent, help us to resurrect the glory of
>   your creation
> for our children and our children's children.
>
> M. Palmer and A. Nash (eds), *Advent and Ecology*,
> WWF, BBC 1988

The following prayer is suitable for Pentecost.

Come Holy Spirit,
  enter our silences.
Come Holy Spirit,
  Into the depths of our longing.
Come Holy Spirit,
  our friend and our lover.
Come Holy Spirit,
  unmask our pretending.
Come Holy Spirit,
  expose our lives.
Come Holy Spirit,
  sustain our weakness.
Come Holy Spirit,
  redeem our creation.

Enter our trusting,
enter our fearing,
enter our letting go,
enter our holding back.

Flood our barren spaces,
make fertile our deserts within.
Break and heal us,
liberator of our desires.

Come Holy Spirit,
  embrace and free us. Amen

Written in Oxford by Neill Thew in 1990

- Try writing a prayer for the Christmas and Easter season, using the above examples as guidelines in bringing together themes from creation and the particular season in the church's year.

2. It draws on prayers which affirm creation in ancient liturgical rites such as those found in the Celtic and Franciscan traditions. Appendix 1 gives an example of the way Celtic liturgy from the Iona Community incorporates creation themes. It is written in the style of the Celtic tradition, but with contemporary concerns and issues in mind.[5]

- What particular prayers would you wish to incorporate in creating a harvest liturgy? For example, try writing your own prayers in the Celtic tradition or the Franciscan tradition.

3. It draws on biblical stories or images through the reinter-pretation of familiar passages or highlighting those passages which have received less attention. The wisdom literature is an example of a neglected resource for liturgical creation. The following prayer is based on Job 38.

O Eternal Wisdom,
who laid the foundations of the earth,
and breathed life into every creature,
creating us in our variety
to cherish your world and seek your face:
we praise you and give you thanks
for your abundant love towards this earth,
violated with our injustice;
and polluted by our sin;
because you took upon you our unprotected flesh,
and entered our struggle;
that you might deliver all creation
from its bondage to oppression and decay.

Therefore, with those whose voice is silenced,
with those who call for freedom,
those whose harvest celebration
sings through hardship and labour and love;
and crying with them for that new creation
when the morning stars shall sing together,
and all the children of God shout for joy,
we praise you, saying:
Holy, holy, holy,
all-creative God,
heaven and earth are full of your glory.
Hosanna in the highest.

Janet Morley in *Till All Creation Sings*, Christian Aid 1989

- Use the Psalms or Proverbs as an inspiration to write your own prayer which you could use in a liturgy for Christmas or Easter or some other season.

4. It pays attention to familiar rhythms, prayers and hymn tunes. If we offer totally new prayers and hymns the absence of memory of such liturgical expressions may be alienating.

- Can you find particular hymns which are evocative for yourself or your community and which are in tune with creation themes?

5. It allows for the existing liturgical structure in different church communities. The Anglican churches, for example, have a regular practice of reciting collects and seasonal sentences; Methodists an 'offertory prayer' and so on. The form and style of prayers are important if they are likely to become part of the regular liturgical practice of the church. In 1989 the Orthodox church through the Ecumenical Patriarchate has declared 1 September as the day to commemorate the gift of creation and pray for the protection of the natural environment. A special liturgy has now been written for use on 1 September in churches throughout the Orthodox world.

- Try writing an outline plan of an advent/other celebration which takes into account your particular church tradition.

6. It recognizes the place for special rites which have as their explicit function the celebration of harvest.

- What special rites does your church community offer for the celebration of harvest? Do you think this celebration is still relevant today?

7. It encourages us to value the material world. If we use wholesome bread in the eucharist instead of wafer thin hosts, it might help to remind us of the material origin of bread and the physical suffering of Christ. The indirect message of the use of wafer hosts is that material existence is to be rejected in favour of an ethereal existence. By using bread which is more wholesome we begin to foster an attitude of affirmation towards creation instead of its rejection.

- Discuss whether we should introduce bread other than wafers to the eucharistic celebration. Do you think we can change the wine to something else, such as grape juice?

8. It is sensitive to the issue of inclusive language. Liturgies are creations of the whole community. They need, therefore, to endeavour to reflect the positive use of inclusive language, taking into account the particular readiness of the community to welcome this language.[6]

- How far might it be possible to introduce inclusive language into liturgical celebrations in your own community?

- Are there limits to the extent of change to inclusive language that you consider is valid and appropriate?

- Discuss the advantages and disadvantages of these changes.

(b) The possible difficulties

There are a number of areas of possible difficulty in formation of a liturgy that is ecological. These include:

1. A sentimentalization of nature from within a lifestyle that is out of touch with it. For example, if we just talk about the 'harmony' in nature and ignore the parasitism, suffering, and death we have an overly romantic picture of the reality of nature.

- Explore how you could counter this tendency in writing your own liturgy.

2. A failure to link our concern for the environment with injustice with respect to human access to the land. It is easy, for example, to think good thoughts about the preservation of species such as whales or pandas, but unless we deal with the concrete issues which affect the just distribution of land rights or wealth we are ignoring the hard implications within the human community itself.

- Explore how you could counter this tendency in writing your own liturgy.

3. A liturgy which addresses 'green' issues in isolation from the mainstream Christian liturgical celebrations. This is the

danger of exclusive use of liturgies designed purely to celebrate creation themes. The harvest festival is an appropriate time of the liturgical year to draw out themes of creation, as shown in Appendix 1.

• Explore how you could counter this tendency in writing your own liturgy.

Note: creation themes can also become embedded in celebrations from different parts of the liturgical calendar.

4. A use of tribal prayers and words in a way which fails to do justice to the particular cultural context from which these prayers have emerged. Sometimes use of prayers from another context in total isolation from its setting can seem patronizing and more like tokenism. In a different cultural setting it can also convey a different meaning.

• Explore how you could counter this tendency in writing your own liturgy.

5. A focus on the confession of ecological sin in a way which leaves an attitude of paralysis and despair. The whole movement of the liturgy needs to be taken into account when we are writing new liturgies. We need to move beyond a focus on misconduct to a point of freedom, hope and resurrection.

• Explore how you could counter this tendency in writing your own liturgy.

6. A failure to acknowledge that not all our theological ideas need to be included in the prayers. In other words our prayers are often more cogent if they are short and simple.

• Explore how you could counter this tendency in writing your own liturgy.

The following prayer is an example of one that is powerful in its simplicity.

Open your eyes and see . . .
God is where the farmer is tilling the hard ground
and where the labourer is breaking stones.

He is with them in the sun and the rain
and his garment is covered with dust.
Put off your holy cloak
and like him come down on to the dusty soil.

from 'The Hidden God' by Rabindranath Tagore

- Turn to the outline plan of a liturgy created for your own community under (a) above. 'Fill out' this liturgy with more details, taking into account the points raised above.

The liturgies that we create do not have to be polished products for use in large-scale worship in church settings. They can help us become more aware of the way our faith can come alive in quite informal groups. The practice of coming together in small groups for Bible study can be complemented by using the opportunity for experiments in liturgy. I have shown throughout this chapter how the themes and concerns of the environmental crisis can begin to be woven into liturgies. These explorations in new ways of corporate worship are not always possible in established liturgies of particular denominations. However, they can give us insights into how these established liturgies could incorporate new elements. They can also help us develop a fresh approach to personal, more private prayer for both individuals and families.

7

Ecology and *Gaia*

1. Introduction to *Gaia*

The *Gaia* hypothesis is one of the more recent developments in the interface between science/religion/spirituality. I refer here to the idea pioneered by James Lovelock in the early 1970s. James Lovelock began his scientific career as an inventor of new technology. He discovered a way of measuring minute quantities of chemicals by means of a device known as an electron capture detector. His discovery allowed him to become increasingly conscious of the spread of minute quantities of toxic substances such as pesticides 'from penguins in Antarctica to the milk of nursing mothers in the United States'. His scientific pursuits then moved into the area of space exploration and the search for life on Mars. He realized that the atmosphere surrounding a life-bearing planet would be radically different from that surrounding a dead planet. In the course of his research Lovelock arrived at the startling conclusion that the atmosphere surrounding the earth must be manipulated by life itself. The alternative is that life has only adapted to the changing conditions of the atmosphere. Lovelock realized that the temperature and gaseous composition of the earth had remained relatively constant for over 3,500 million years. This seemed to him to suggest that life kept these conditions constant as well as adapted to environmental conditions, rather than the alternative that life only adapted to fluctuations.

Lovelock devised a scheme for the way the total life processes on earth could manipulate the environment. He called this scheme the *Gaia* hypothesis, a name suggested by William

Golding, the poet. The name *Gaia* is that of the ancient Greek goddess of the earth. It seemed to Lovelock at the time that using the same name for his hypothesis was a fitting way to describe the powerful force that seemed to have operated for so many millennia. The difference between accepted scientific dogma and Lovelock's ideas is that the planet is not envisaged as something dead and inert with living things on it, but that the whole planet is *alive*. The non-living parts of the planet such as atmospheric gases function rather like the dead bark of a tree in the sense that they are an integral part of the living system as a whole. In other words the living organisms, also known as the *biota*, and atmosphere function as a single unit in the same way that the bark of a tree is still part of the whole organism.

This seems to be an interesting paradox. Those who were responsible for polluting industries immediately realized that *Gaia* might give them a rationale for their action. *Gaia* as a self-regulating device that had survived so many millennia would certainly be able to cope with the output of chemicals from industrialization. Not all would agree with this conclusion since the rate of change caused by human activity has become accelerated to such an extent that the long-term stability of the whole system is threatened. Hence others, including many ecologists, saw in *Gaia* a rather different message. For them *Gaia* represented a move away from the objective, detached and mechanical science to one that is more sensitive to treating the earth as a whole. If we interfere with *Gaia's* workings through careless human intervention it might have devastating consequences.

2. The relationship between *Gaia* and ecology

Lovelock is not the first scientist who has considered that the earth might function as an organism. James Hutton, an eighteenth-century Scottish scientist and V. Vernadsky, a Russian scientist, writing at the turn of the century, also believed that the earth was alive. Overall, however, the philosophy of René

Descartes (1596–1650), who likened the earth to a machine, became the more accepted working hypothesis of the eighteenth and nineteenth centuries. The mechanistic philosophy also tried to explain the harmony in the universe, but now the processes were seen to be automatic and mechanical.

- Discuss the possible implications of the organismic model of the earth compared with the mechanistic model.

The discrete science of ecology developed later in the twentieth century. It deliberately set out to discover the basis for the inter-relationships between living beings and their natural environment. The early idea in the eighteenth and nineteenth centuries was that there was a 'balance' of nature, but one that could be upset by human intervention. Organisms were known to have some effect on their environment. For example, in 1877 T. H. Huxley noticed the importance of plants in reducing levels of carbon dioxide in the atmosphere. By the twentieth century ecologists sought to quantify the relationship between different species and their environment in terms of a mutual dependence of energy relations.

More recently, ecologists have questioned the idea that eco-systems display long-term stability. On the other hand, ecosystems are not so fragile that the whole system is thrown into convulsions by any change. Ecology has been called a 'subversive' science because it assumes that the sum of the parts has properties which the elements lack. A traditional scientist believes that anything which cannot be explained in terms of physics and chemistry and ultimately mathematics is not really 'hard science'. Ecologists are more often those scientists who believe that the system as a whole has unique properties.

The *Gaia* hypothesis is, in a sense, a development of the organic ideal followed by ecologists. It goes further in suggesting that not only do organisms co-exist in ecological webs, but that all the interacting webs connect in a giant system that is subject to regulation by the living parts. In this sense *Gaia* has evolved as a way of helping life as a whole to survive.

- Is the planet alive? What do we mean by 'life' in this context?

Theoretical problems surface once we start asking questions about the kind of mechanism by which *Gaia* as a homeostatic system could evolve. I will discuss these scientific questions in a later section. More important, perhaps, is that *Gaia* provides a *world-view* that encourages the search for relationships between organic and inorganic life and in this sense ecology is extended to geology, climatology, oceanology and a number of other disciplines. Ecology on its own does not encourage such bold steps into other subject areas. *Gaia* as a way of perceiving the world or *myth* will have done us a service if it has succeeded in breaking down the specialisms in science. Other theological and ethical problems arise if we allow *Gaia* to be the foundation for philosophy based on ecology. More radical ecologists have, in their search for greater justification for their views, encouraged ecology to become a complete way of seeing the world and giving meaning to our existence. If *Gaia* becomes part of such a trend it takes on powers which have ethical consequences. I will unravel this question in greater detail later.

3. Roots of *Gaia* in the goddess myth

One of the reasons why some scientists were reluctant to take Lovelock seriously was the seeming connection between his hypothesis and early ideas of an earth goddess. This connection, however, fascinated the public and allowed him a greater hearing than might have been possible if he had used a different name. No one would have been excited if he had called his idea something like *The Geophysiology Hypothesis*. Also it would have betrayed the vagueness of some of his definitions, a point I will return to later. The fascination of *Gaia* is that it captures the imagination and specifically the *religious* instinct of those who hear about the idea. The most obvious is that *Gaia* finds echoes in ancient religious views of a goddess which are an integral part of the archetypal ideas that have existed for many thousands of years. Other religious ideas evoked by *Gaia* are mystical beliefs in the interconnectedness of all things, which now seems to have a material basis.

Gaia, or more accurately *Gaea*, or *Ge*, was the primaeval earth deity of ancient Greece. She was the fruitful power sustaining universal life and the common ancestress of all the gods and demigods in the Greek theogony. *Ge* is never wholly personal, even though she bears offspring. Some of her offspring were unfathered, such as *Pontus* and *Uranus*, the personifications of the sea and heavens respectively. *Ge* is by essence a generative deity who is ever renewing life, and is associated with her offspring *Demeter*, who takes on her characteristic of fertility. However, the earth Mother is not always a compassionate figure. In common with other ancient goddesses, she has a shadow side and can be the unforgiving and stern bringer of death.

Lovelock's *Gaia* is no exception to this double imagery. To use Lovelock's own words *Gaia* keeps the world 'warm and comfortable for those who obey the rules, but is ruthless in her destruction of those who transgress'. Lovelock relates *Gaia* both to these ancient ideas about Mother Earth and to the devotion to the Virgin Mary. He asks:

> What if Mary is another name for *Gaia*? Then her capacity for virgin birth is no miracle or parthenogenetic aberration; it is a role of *Gaia* since life began . . . Any living organism a quarter as old as the Universe itself and still full of vigour is as near immortal as we ever need to know. She is of this Universe and, conceivably, a part of God.

James Lovelock, *The Ages of Gaia*, OUP 1979

- The above quote illustrates how science can take on religious language. Do you think this is:
  (i) Confusing?
  (ii) Helping to heal the split between science and religion?
  (iii) Unwarranted speculation?

4. The challenge of *Gaia* to biblical and theological interpretations of cosmology

An understanding of the earth according to a biblical perspective is that according to Genesis 1.1 it is created by God and in the beginning was 'formless and empty'. The idea of consciousness is restricted to human beings. When *Gaia* draws on ancient images of a world soul it seems to give the earth a quality of consciousness. I will take the idea of consciousness up again in the section on ethics below. The biblical idea of consciousness comes through both God, as distinct creator and sustainer of the earth, and humanity made in God's image.

The traditional theological interpretation of Genesis is that God is distinct from the world and created the world out of nothing. God pre-exists before the world comes into existence. If we shift our understanding of God so that there is less distinction between God and the world it becomes easier to accommodate the idea that God and *Gaia* are part of each other in the manner hinted at by Lovelock above. A radical view of God is that the world is God's body, which makes God's transcendence of the world similar to a human person's transcendence of their body. The experience and suffering of the world has an effect on the experience and suffering of God. This is very different from the traditional view of God's providence over creation which draws on biblical passages such as Heb. 1.3 and Acts 17.28. The traditional view is that God exists in relationship with creation, rather than God emerges from creation. (For a further discussion of God's transcendence, see chapter 4 on Ecology, Women and Christian Community.)

There have been some more liberal theologians who have welcomed Lovelock's thesis as a way of reinforcing their understanding of God who exists in terms of interconnected relationships. In other words, a particular feature of the *Gaia* hypothesis, namely that of the interconnectedness of the planet, is taken up and used in theological models of God. There are other more controversial aspects of *Gaia* which theologians have to accept in order to draw closer parallels between process thought and *Gaia*. Process theology gives all creation a *directedness* or *teleology*. This directedness is one of the ways that creation shapes God in his *consequent* being. Lovelock and many other scientists do not accept formally that *Gaia* has a direction or goal. The idea of teleology in science is unacceptable to traditional scientists who insist that chance rather than advance planning is responsible for the emergence of life. My first point is that we can only link *Gaia* with process theology if we assume that *Gaia* is goal-directed.

My second point is that the teleologies of *Gaia* and process thought are distinct. The directedness of creation in process theology is always orientated towards good or the Divine Eros. The teleology in *Gaia* is more ambiguous, as it is towards the survival of life. The use of *Gaia* by process theologians does not distinguish adequately between these different teleologies, that in process thought towards the ultimate good, and that in *Gaia* towards the survival of life. As far as the *Gaia* hypothesis is concerned human survival has no priority. Not all process theologians welcome Lovelock's ideas, since they recognize that he resists the idea of teleology, as I will explain further below. They object to Lovelock's insistence that the process of regulation of environmental conditions happens automatically. His understanding of teleology is a weak one, that is the maintenance of life is a by-product of the system, rather than a result of any advance planning. Other process theologians regard his views as too narrow a cosmology confined, as it is, to planet earth.

The above shows that while Lovelock's ideas have been welcomed by some more liberal theologians, the use of his ideas has been highly selective. For example, consider the apparent prominence given to micro-organisms in Lovelock's scheme. These organisms are largely responsible for keeping the environmental conditions on earth constant. If we look at the order of creation given in Genesis, the story seems to suggest a special blessing on higher animals and humanity. According to *Gaia* the ordering is not simply egalitarian, but is inverted. Those feminist theologians who have drawn on Lovelock as inspiration for a more egalitarian approach have ignored this prominence of microbes.

- Discuss the role of human responsibility according to Lovelock's hypothesis. Can you reconcile this with the biblical theology expressed in Genesis 1 and 2?

- How else does Lovelock's theory challenge Christian thought?

More conservative theologians worry that Lovelock's ideas promote and encourage a New Age spirituality. The earth goddess of pagan thought comes to the surface in a new form, namely Lovelock's hypothesis. Lovelock categorically denies that his ideas provide an object for religious worship. However, he remarks that in his childhood he thought of Christmas more like a solstice feast and as a family they were 'amazingly superstitious'. His comments like these have encouraged New Age thinkers to use Lovelock's ideas to support their position. It is paradoxical, perhaps, that one of the New Age ideals of human self-fulfilment and individual self-improvement does not sit easily with the concept of the world as a single organism, apparently oblivious to individual or human interests. This may be one of the reasons why Lovelock's views have not had a whole-hearted welcome among New Age thinkers. Another problem as far as they are concerned is that Lovelock deliberately tries to give evidence for his hypothesis according to scientific methods. New Age thinkers can still draw on the ancient ideas of the goddess without referring to Lovelock's work. For some New Age thinkers Lovelock seems to be too conforming to the scientific establishment. However, as I will show below, his views are controversial amongst scientists.

Those theologians who are more conservative can only incorporate Lovelock's ideas if they adopt one of the *less* controversial forms of his hypothesis. I will be giving an outline of these different versions of the hypothesis below.

- Discuss whether there are elements of Lovelock's hypothesis which are consistent with more traditional theology.

For example, to invoke *Gaia* as part of *God's plan* for the creation of life we would have to suggest that *Gaia* is the working of the Holy Spirit. It is difficult to argue that God the Holy Spirit is responsible for *Gaia* when there are so many different versions of the hypothesis. Which version should we take as the blueprint for the wise designer? Moreover, there are negative undercurrents in the hypothesis which are whitewashed by a link between a wise Creator God and his wise design. Alternatively, if we allow these undercurrents to exist, we are forced to modify our understanding of the future of creation as good. The future of creation according to *Gaia* is one which may or may not include human beings. In this scenario the goodness of creation seems to be independent of human existence.

- Discuss the challenge of *Gaia* to a biblical understanding of human beings made in the image of God

We arrive at the surprising conclusion that *Gaia* can be used by a number of different theologians to support their own understanding of God and creation. For some feminist theologians *Gaia* reinforces the idea that the world and God are one interconnected being. For some New Age thinkers this hypothesis is a revival of the wisdom of the ancient earth goddess. For a few more conservative theologians *Gaia* is part of the divine design of the world. The acceptance of these ideas even within these groups is variable and seems to be subject to individual preference.

- Do you think *Gaia* is the right word to use for Lovelock's hypothesis?

- Discuss different ways *Gaia* can be used under the following headings. *Gaia* as goddess, *Gaia* as Mother Earth, *Gaia* as world view, *Gaia* as preserver of life, *Gaia* as interdependent relationships. Are all these different aspects of *Gaia* compatible?

5. Is *Gaia* refuted or supported by science?

I have hinted earlier that one of the difficulties with *Gaia* is that it can mean many different things to different people. It is supported by polluters and 'deep' ecologists, to name two groups. Examples of how this difference arises become clearer if we do what at first sight seems to be foreign to *Gaian* thinking, that is subdivide the different strands within *Gaia* to show how it is possible to come up with widely differing views.

(a) *Influential* Gaia

According to this view life on the planet has an *influence* over
certain aspects of the non-living world, such as temperature and
composition of the atmosphere. In this sense the sum total of life
on the planet is active in the 'regulation' of its environment. This
is the least radical form of *Gaia* in that it asks us to make the least
number of assumptions. It is accepted generally by scientists.
Although the classical view is that organisms adapt to their
environment, scientists have recognized that they also influence
external conditions in some way.

(b) *Co-evolutionary or evolutionary* Gaia

Here the *biota* influences the non-living world which in turn
influences the evolution of the living organisms as two functions
of one system acting in concert. The *biota*, defined as the sum
total of living things, has supposedly *co-evolved* along with its
environment.

We have to assume first that the earth evolved as a whole. This
is difficult to imagine from a genetic standpoint as it would
involve the genes of a range of species acting in concert to keep
conditions constant. How could such a system be said to *evolve*
when there is no alternative? The word evolution begs the
question of how *Gaia* can be selected since there are no
alternatives with which to test the chance of survival. Usually
organisms evolve by a process of selection of the genes which are
best suited to the survival of the species. Those organisms which
are less well adapted to their environment die earlier and produce
less offspring than those organisms which are well adapted.
Evolutionary *Gaia* is more accurately the emergence or development of mutual interaction between living and non-living components of the planet. Even if we accept the idea of the
development of *Gaia* it becomes very difficult to envisage how
such a system could develop according to classical genetics. The
ideal external conditions of temperature, gaseous composition
and so on for one organism may not be right for another.

- *Gaia* challenges scientific specialization and compartmentalization. Discuss the way it challenges belief in a remote, masculine God.

(c) *Homeostatic* Gaia

Here the *biota* influence their external environment in a way that keeps the external conditions constant. The process works through a *negative feedback* mechanism. As the temperature increases, for example, the *biota* sense the change in conditions. They respond by absorbing more heat radiation and bringing down the temperature. Lovelock put forward a simplified theoretical model of just daisies on the earth or *Daisyworld* to show how this could happen. In this model there are two populations of daisies, white ones which reflect heat and have a high optimal temperature for growth, and black ones which absorb heat with a lower optimal temperature. As the temperature of the planet rises, more white daisies grow and their reflection lowers the temperature. A similar situation exists with black daisies except that they are more abundant in lower temperatures. How can we find empirical proof that stabilizing systems are dominant? There is a 50% chance that organisms will be found to have a stabilizing effect on the environment simply according to the law of averages. While this model at first sight seems to answer the critics, we arrive at another problem. That is the comparison is always made between the theory and predicted outcome of that theory, rather than the theory and empirical data. We could quite easily construct a different model. Consider another theoretical hypothetical model such as 'Lupinworld'. Here we have an association of lupins and micro-organisms. At higher temperatures the microbes grow at a faster rate than the lupins, and produce more carbon dioxide than can be used by the higher plants during photosynthesis. This increase in carbon dioxide would then increase the temperature further via the greenhouse effect. In this model the *biota* have a *destabilizing* effect on the climate.

Gaian protagonists have searched for stabilizing mechanisms, but have not looked for destabilizing mechanisms. Until there is some idea of the relative dominance of stabilizing mechanisms there is little hard evidence for the living systems as a whole operating to keep external conditions constant.

- Discuss the idea of *Gaia* under the following headings: *Gaia* as mechanical feedback, *Gaia* as geophysiology. In the light of the scientific discussion do you have anything to add to the idea of Gaia as interdependent relationships? Are these different aspects of *Gaia* compatible with each other and with the first list drawn up at the end of section 4?

(d) Teleological Gaia

The homeostatic idea outlined above is enlarged so that the atmosphere and so on is not just kept constant, but is kept constant for a *purpose*: that is the benefit of the *biota* and the continuation of life. The purpose of *Gaia* is the creation of an environment that is favourable for life. This begs the question: how can conditions be optimal for micro-organisms, penguins, chimpanzees all at the same time? There are bound to be some losers!

Some of Lovelock's earliest critics were severe in their accusation that he was 'teleological'. He argued that the system works by itself and attempted to prove this by coming up with a model called 'Daisyworld' outlined under (c) above. Lovelock argued that this proves that *Gaia* is not teleological; rather it works automatically.

The other evidence that has been cited in support of *Gaia* are various schemes which show cycling of sulphur, oxygen, carbon dioxide. I will cite one of the better documented examples by way of illustration. Certain marine phytoplankton produce a gas known as dimethylsulphide (DMS), which encourages the formation of cloud droplets. The greater the number of droplets, the more reflective the cloud. As the temperature rises DMS production increases and the increase in cloud density leads to less of the sun's rays reaching the surface and a consequent lowering of the temperature.

The problem here is that we do not always find the expected relationship between production of DMS by the marine organisms and cloud density. This evidence supports the idea that organisms have an effect on the environment. However, it has not proved that these organisms control temperature for their benefit or that of all living creatures through DMS production.

Overall it seems that while we can test scientifically for the operation of *Gaian* mechanisms in a limited sense, it is very difficult to test for the more global aspects of the theory. Most scientists consider that theories which cannot be tested are unhelpful because we can never arrive at empirical evidence for such a theory. If we find evidence for *Gaia* in its weak form, such as that outlined for DMS production above, and use it to support teleological forms of *Gaia*, it is against the basic principles of science. We can then ask a further question: if this is not science, does this hypothesis fit in with other forms of experience? In this case *Gaia* is still a useful metaphor or myth. It challenges science to be more holistic.

- Are there two *Gaias*, a scientific hypothesis and a myth? Or do both intertwine? How does this affect the morality of *Gaia*?

6. The significance of *Gaia* for environmental ethics

Gaia not only fits into a number of different scientific models, it also can lead to a wide diversity of ethical standpoints.

(a) Gaia *as Moral*

According to this perspective the co-operation and integration that is basic to the way *Gaia* works becomes the model for human behaviour.

The living history of the planet has shown that larger life forms are only relatively recent occupants of the earth. For many millennia the bacteria and monocellular organisms dominated the earth's history. As far as *Gaia* is concerned its stability is largely dependent on the activity of micro-organisms. Larger organisms, including humans, are rather like parasites on the planet. The moral of *Gaia* is that unless we choose to become more co-operative with the rest of the planet we will disappear.

Human beings are like experiments in free choice. Unlike other species we are not biologically programmed to know what to do. This gives us an enormous potential to be self-centred. It also gives us a tremendous sense of anxiety since we have within our decisions the power to effect change. In order for humans to survive we have to work with rather than against *Gaia*.

- Do you find this argument convincing? Discuss the potential difficulties with this view.

(b) Gaia *as Immoral*

There is a possibility that if we use *Gaia* as a guide for ethical principles this will have *immoral* rather than moral consequences. If *Gaia* aims to survive at any cost it becomes selfish rather than altruistic. *Gaia* is indifferent to nuclear war and human self-destruction. Indeed *Gaia*, if 'she' is conscious, might see this as a convenient way of reducing human population so that the rest of the planet can survive.

- Discuss the assumptions implicit in this model. Is it fair to call *Gaia* immoral?

- Do you think we can blame *Gaia* for the extinction of species?

(c) Gaia *as Amoral*

Gaia as amoral means that 'it' has no moral principles and cannot be judged by moral values. 'It' operates blind, as it were, to human values, or any value system at all. Those scientists that are part of the establishment would tend to adopt this view, since they would reject teleological *Gaia* and presuppose that facts can be separate from values. In this instance not only is *Gaia* amoral, 'it' is outside moral consideration.

- Discuss the possibility that we can take a completely detached view of *Gaia*. What are the practical implications?

It seems to me that the powerful images that *Gaia* provokes make it unlikely that it can be neutralized and contained in scientific terms. An alternative view is that even if *Gaia* is amoral, it is still worth *moral consideration*. The practical result of this interpretation is that even human behaviour becomes caught up in the meaningless dance of the universe. We become powerless in the face of *Gaia* who is neither good nor bad, but aimless. *Gaia* is certainly not neutral in its effects. Rather it has added to our sense of meaninglessness in the universe.

(d) Other ethical implications

Gaia as moral, or amoral in the second sense above, challenges us to extend our system of values so that the earth as a whole becomes a centre of value. Traditionally we have taken guidelines for moral behaviour as the values which have emerged after generations of human experience. For example, if we have a choice between saving a dog or saving a human life, in most circumstances most of us are bound to save human life. This approach to ethics is centred around human behaviour and is *anthropocentric* in orientation. Here moral value is something we attribute solely to human beings. Only human beings have value in and of themselves or *intrinsic* value. Such *intrinsic* value may be extended to animals, in which case we move from a position of *anthropocentrism* to *biocentrism*. Once we argue that a system as a whole has value we are putting the centre of value beyond the human community. The approach now is *holistic*. In other words it is not so much an extension of human values to animals and life as in biocentrism, but finding a new locus of value altogether. (For further discussion see chapter 5 on Ecology and Ethics).

The strongest view of *Gaia*, which gives it a purpose, makes it relatively easy to adopt the view that *Gaia* has intrinsic value. Nonetheless, even *Gaia* as just a living system could have intrinsic value. The difficulty now is that the earth is not 'alive' in the accepted biological sense. The latter would require that we accept that it has emerged by evolution, has internal homeostasis, can grow and reproduce and is capable of death. The property of homeostasis is shared by computers and cars. Cybernetics, or the study of control systems, is also an aspect of engineering. If we argue that *Gaia* has intrinsic value because it is alive, we are changing the meaning of life and the definition of intrinsic value.

Does *Gaia* have a sense of consciousness? There are a number of different positions we could adopt. We might take the view that it has no consciousness. Any idea that *Gaia* is a threat to human survival becomes imaginary rather than real. In a weak form *Gaian* consciousness could mean little more than the persistence of life. This seems to be the view adopted by Lovelock. In this case the threat posed by some life forms, such as humans, on the overall persistence of the planet are such that *Gaia* reacts strongly to correct such threats. A more extreme view is that *Gaia's* consciousness has evolved and at its highest form human beings have appeared. In this case we become like the eye of the planet; the self-awareness of the planet is possible through humanity.

• How far can we attribute consciousness, personality, purpose and ultimately spirituality to *Gaia*? If 'she' is a spiritual being, is this the power behind 'her' force as a moral being?

We now arrive at a paradox in the *Gaia* myth:

On the one hand human beings are like the nervous system of the earth, that which operates to coordinate the different activities of the body. During the development of the earth we could expect humans to increase in numbers, rather like the rapid multiplication of neurons in the brain. In a sense the bigger the brain, the better for the health of the whole organism. The implication now is that we should not be threatened by the population explosion. Humans facilitate the coordination of all the different activities of the body. However, most of these functions would be outside the direct decision-making by humans, and hence would be unconscious.

On the other hand human beings could be the unwanted species, the cancerous growth in the organism which sooner or later has to be cut out for the sake of the whole. The worst action that humans can take now is to assume responsibility for the planet, and become 'managers' of the planet. Instead of allowing the planet to regulate itself, in its disabled state the planet requires 'management'. Life no longer becomes carefree as in the normal workings of a healthy planetary body where such functions were largely unconscious. As it is for a person with malfunctioning organs, day to day living is stressful and a battle for survival.

The lesson of both these images is that given our own failure to manage ourselves, we shift final responsibility to the planet. This is both a relief and an anxiety. If we believe that *Gaia* is moral then we can rest assured that by working with it we will arrive at a healthier and more advanced planet. We just need to 'grow up' a little and conform to 'her' ways. On the other hand if we believe that *Gaia* is immoral or amoral what kind of guarantees do we have that our future is in any way part of its future? The threat of possible action by *Gaia* leads now to a sense of paralysis in human action and responsibility.

8

Ecology and Politics

1. Green issues as part of politics and political theology

It is significant, perhaps, that green issues have only relatively late in our history come to dominate the specifically political agenda. The emergence of the Green Party and other organizations such as Friends of the Earth in the 1970s have acted as pressure groups to raise public concern and ultimately political consciousness. It is a good example of the way the political agenda can be shifted through the actions of grass roots movements. Another recent development is that the ecological problems have now become so acute that these issues are taken seriously right across the political spectrum. We can expect, then, considerable diversity of opinion in 'green' politics. For example, the more established political parties would view environmental issues as another contemporary issue which has a political dimension. The basic political values and aims remain intact. On the other hand, the political groups that are less established might use green issues as a means to promote change in other areas of policy-making. A third position is where green issues themselves take centre stage as the fundamental political question around which we need to fit other agenda. The latter two groups are radical in their political views, whereas the first group would be in favour of a modification of the existing established structure, rather than their replacement.

• Refer to the reporting of environmental issues in three different newspapers which have a different political bias. Do you find any differences in the way the events were recorded? What conclusions do you come to? Repeat the same exercise using newspapers in your local library ten years ago. What differences are there in the coverage of environmental issues? (Look at amount of coverage, tone, amount of knowledge assumed.)

There is an increasing awareness that Christianity does have a political face. However, this can be a threat to those who consider that Christian and spiritual issues should be divorced from political action. The latter argue that the purpose of Christianity is to promote the devotional life of individuals and is in the private domain of personal decision. Those who accept that Christianity does have a political dimension believe that our values need to be incorporated into the political structure of the society and not just kept within the private sphere. For them, the question is not so much whether Christianity is relevant, but the nature of the dialogue between theology and politics. The purpose of this chapter is to highlight particular ecological issues in this dialogue.

In the last quarter of a century theology has become more self-conscious of this political dimension, though in general political theology is understood to mean theology biased towards the socialist politics of the left. The justification for this view is that such a stance is a necessary prerequisite for truly Christian theology. The history of Jesus' life shows that he did not align himself with the powerful in society, but with those without political or religious authority. He challenged the status quo within the Jewish community itself and so went further than the zealots who were concerned to liberate the Jews from Roman oppression. Albert Nolan comments:

> Jesus set out to liberate Israel from Rome by persuading Israel to change. Without a change in heart within Israel itself, liberation from imperialism of any kind would have been impossible. That had been the message of all the prophets, including John the Baptist. Jesus was a prophet and he was involved in politics in exactly the same way as all the prophets had been . . .
>
> The revolution that Jesus wanted to bring about was far more radical than anything the Zealots or anyone else might have had in mind. Every sphere of life, political, economic, social and religious, was radically questioned by Jesus and turned upside down. Current ideas about what was right and

just were shown to be loveless and therefore contrary to the
will of God.

Albert Nolan, *Jesus Before Christianity: The Gospel of
Liberation*, Darton, Longman and Todd 1976

- Do you think that theology has the right to become explicitly
  political in this way?

- Do you think we can apply the above political theology to our
  situation in the West? What are the changes you would suggest?

- Do you think that the above theology has a universal appeal? Who
  gets left out of a theology which is explicitly biased to the poor?
  What do you think are some of the reasons for and against political
  theology becoming normative for the world-wide church?

As I hinted above, there are signs that theology can have a
political edge within a more established view. The biblical sources
in this case are more likely to be Pauline, where he recommends
submission to authorities as in Romans 13. In this way theology
can be used to *legitimate* existing structures. The challenge is to
discern whether Christian principles are being shaped by political
ideology and then used to promote this ideology.

It is fair to say that the temptation for Christian theology has
been to opt too often for identification with the status quo and by
its passivity endorse the prevailing social structures. In the early
stages of its formation political theology was a reaction against
this passivity and was perhaps rather too inclined to baptize left-
wing politics without an adequate sense of detachment from their
presuppositions. The broad fields on which political theology cut
its teeth were in the writings of Bonhoeffer, Niebuhr and post-
war Christian/Marxist dialogue and emergent theologies of hope,
revolution, development, liberation and black theology.

The expression *liberation theology* was first used in Latin
America. This theology is one which aims to show the poor the
roots of their oppression through a process known as *consci-
entization*, that is, becoming conscious of their own situation.
Liberation theologians were determined to develop their theo-

logy in the light of their practical situation of poverty. The idea of *praxis* is practical action informed by a particular theory, which in turn is influenced by practice. They believed that theology should emerge from 'below', from the experience of oppression. Theology should, in addition, become detached from the dominance of Western ideas which they believe legitimate existing oppressive social structures. In other words, liberation theology is one developed from the current situation, rather than beginning with defined dogmas handed down by the hierarchical authority. The starting point for this theology is the *experience* of ordinary people, rather than dogmatics. Further, as one might expect in the Roman Catholic church, the liberation theologies emerging from Latin America were in considerable tension with the Vatican. While the liberation theologians made every effort to be faithful to Catholic tradition, their theology was perceived as having too much bias in the direction of Marxist politics. It was feared that liberation theology would be used to legitimate revolution using proof texts taken from Exodus and the New Testament where Christ is portrayed as the Liberator. It was therefore deemed unacceptable as a theology fit for the universal church. Nonetheless, the importance and influence of liberation theology in challenging theology to be more in touch with political issues and structural sin is undeniable.

Jürgen Moltmann is a Protestant theologian who was one of the pioneers of political theology through his *Theology of Hope*.[1] This theology challenges the structures of society and looks towards a liberated future kingdom which comes from a God of the future. He recognized the need for theology to include a challenge to the scientific technological structures of Western society. He believed that in the Western world technological structures have become a trap for both human beings and creation. In the past liberation theologians have tended to view the green movement with suspicion, believing that the primary task must be the liberation of people, rather than the preservation of non-human species. However, the *global* effects of the environmental crisis and the interconnection between development and environment mean that these two issues can no longer be considered in isolation. I will be coming back to this issue again in the next chapter. In Moltmann's more recent work he lays emphasis on how the theology of hope extends to include the liberation of the suffering, dying planet, which is an example of human oppression *par excellence*. In this sense political theology becomes ecological political theology.

2. Political theology in the Bible

The interaction between scripture and politics is an area of much debate. The early political theologies were in danger of using themes of liberation in the Old and New Testament as proof texts for their views. On the other hand, the genuine political implications of the Bible stories become more obvious once we start looking for political issues which underlie the context in which these stories were written. There is always the danger of manipulating the text to support our preconceived attitudes. In this way it can become a source of justification for our political views, rather than a challenge. By listening to the way liberation theologians of the Third World interpret the Bible we can become more sensitive to the way the Bible sounds to those Christians persecuted by oppressive regimes. This counters some of the tendency to listen to the Bible in a way which fosters our own self-interest. We also need to take into account the difference between the historical cultural context of the Bible story and our present context in order to avoid too simplistic application.

Case study: Psalm 10

Psalm 10 and its interpretation illustrates the way the Bible can be interpreted in a way which draws out its political implications.

The psalm is a cry from the depth of despair and oppression, a complaint against God, who has left the people to suffer.

The enemies represent a situation of social conflict, and the psalmist demands revenge for this oppression of the poor by the wicked. The wicked are those who pursue profit to the exclusion of everything else (v. 3).

The poor are those vulnerable in their sense of powerlessness, emphasized by the image of the net used by the wicked to trap the poor. The poor are oppressed, exploited (v. 18) and like orphans, that is in a position of social and economic defencelessness (v. 14, 18). The poor have no other means of protection and justice than the God of Israel.

The psalm moves from complaint against God to trust, hope and confidence; though not without first expressing bitterness and protest.

The theology of the Exodus in some respects parallels that of the psalm. We find a similar movement from complaint, God hears, and God delivers.

- Read through the psalm several times and note down your own reactions to it. In what ways are you challenged?

- Think of a specific situation of injustice or of oppression in the world today, and find out as much detail as you can about it. Then rewrite some or all of Psalm 10 from the point of view of the oppressed, inserting specific names, details, actions where relevant. For example: vv. 4–7: What do the oppressed feel is the mental attitude of the oppressor?
  vv. 8–9: What means does the oppressor use?
  vv. 10–11: What happens to the victims? What do they say to themselves?
  v. 15: What would the oppressed like to see happening?

- What does this psalm tell you about the relationship between God and the psalmist? Is the sense of the absence of God equivalent to loss of relationship?

- Rewrite the texts of Ex. 3.7–8 and Deut. 26.7–8 in the light of the situation of injustice that you identified above. What do these passages tell you about the relationship between God and the authors?

- In the light of your study above discuss some of the reasons why the Exodus theme is so important for theologies of liberation.

The connection between God and social justice emerges in Psalm 10, the absence of social justice amounting to the absence of God. The wicked leave God out of their behaviour and in this way are practical atheists, even though the formal denial of the existence of God was not really an intellectual possibility at the time. The wicked are arrogant in their assumption that they can exploit the poor with impunity (vv. 2a, 3–4, 6). The complaint of the psalmist is that it appears that the wicked are correct, that God does not care about the plight of the poor.

The psalm raises the age-old struggle of the existence of evil: how can God be God if God allows this to happen? However, this is no theoretical question: it is in the live and painful context of social evil and oppression. It is a question of survival, a question which makes the address and complaint against God a sign of hope that God can be addressed and that he is aware of injustice. Without this hope the victims would fall prey to despair and the absence of hope.

The psalmist demands an active response to the concrete situation. He pleads for an end to the injustice and retribution for the oppressors. He then affirms that God is the God who responds in the deliverance of the oppressed (v. 14b). This affirmation of the character of God shifts the tenor of the psalm from complaint to assurance.

The psalmist's confidence and hope have already transformed the situation from its more destructive effects. His hope in God gives him a new inner strength to resist in a way that sustains his struggle against injustice. It is no 'opium' for the people, but fosters the spirit of resistance against oppression.

3. Links between political, economic and environmental issues

(a) *The Rio Earth Summit of June 1992*

In June 1992 an international convention was held at Rio in order to arrive at a global response to environmental issues and their interconnectedness with 'development' issues. The latter includes questions about justice within the human community in a way which links in with responsibility for the ecological crisis. The summit attracted more heads of state, official delegations and a larger media presence than any previous international conference. There were a number of important issues raised by the Rio Summit. The conference highlighted the particular links between global environmental problems and poverty. I will outline here the specific issue of how the global response to environmental problems depends on the will of those richer nations involved to make economic sacrifices. A *convention on biological diversity* was signed by 153 governments. The USA refused to sign initially but later agreed under the Clinton administration. The commitment of those who did sign is to set up national monitoring schemes for species conservation, to restore degraded ecosystems and to help endangered species recover. A *Rio Declaration* outlined 27 principles to govern the economic and environmental behaviour of individuals and nations. This fell far short of the Earth Charter hoped for which would have outlined a new global ethic. The Rio Summit included recommendations for a specific programme of action to be taken on issues such as desertification; involvement of women and indigenous peoples in sustainable development; basic human needs such as health, housing and education; protection of the atmosphere and oceans. These recommendations were summarized in a statement called *Agenda 21*. While each country is required to develop a national plan for implementing the agenda, the obligation is a vague one. In order to implement Agenda 21, US$600 billion would be needed per year by 'developing' countries. Calculations showed that the current levels of foreign aid were completely inadequate to meet this quota, so that US$125 billion would have to come from *additional* foreign aid. It was clear that donor governments were not prepared to increase foreign aid by this amount. In other words *economic pressures* were related to a lack of implementation of political decisions. Only US$6–7 billion was pledged at Rio, which is only 5% of the required funds. The South pressed for the Northern richer nations to allocate 0.7% of their Gross National Product (GNP) for foreign aid. This has now become the UN target for the amount of foreign aid to be given by Northern nations to Southern nations. There was no consensus of this commitment. The anger of the Southern nations was that the lifestyles of the richer Northern nations was not even open to question.

Rio highlighted the growing tension between North and South replacing that formerly existing between East and West. The economic difference between East and West is less extreme than that between North and South.

- Set up a debate between an official from an Eastern block country pressing for Western Economic Aid to help in a new business venture and a representative from the Third World insisting that the West helps pay for pollutant control. What did you learn from their discussions?

The failure of the Earth Summit in Rio in June 1992 to make more progress was disappointing in view of the broad interest in ecological and justice issues, but not surprising given the range of opinion as to how to respond to the crisis. The environmental crisis is not simply about the survival of non-human species, but about justice within the human community, the human environment. Not everyone equated the survival of the planet with human survival. Not everyone was prepared for the economic reforms that would be required for real and lasting change.

(b) Political alienation

The experience of the former USSR demonstrates how a political vision of corporate equality becomes detached from the real needs of the people through an over-centralized government. This experience has not been unique to communist regimes. Even in democratic nations over-centralization has legitimized oppression of various marginalized groups deemed to be outside the system.

- As the political machinery becomes more remote how do we combat apathy? What role do you think the church should have in encouraging its members to become politically active?

There are many areas of work which fall outside the current economic system or *market system*. I will develop the theme of the market in more detail below. Examples of unpaid employment include voluntary work, subsistence farming, much women's work in child rearing and so on. The economists' view of progress is to ignore such contributions. However, a more holistic approach is to take special account of these *hidden* factors which shape the economy.

• Those who are less articulate are unlikely to be able to influence policies even at local government level. In this situation how do you think their interests should be represented?

(c) The market economy

The exchange of commodites during fairs and market days is an ancient practice. In this sense the market exists in a range of political structures including communism and feudalism. In these situations it is not the organizing principle of the economy. Once the 'market' becomes the organizing principle of the economy we find a transition between feudalism and bourgeois capitalism. A form of capitalism exists in communist countries, but it is state capitalism which is not sensitive to market forces or driven by individual profit motives. The 'market' is a mechanism by which exchange is enabled to take place by coordinating the interests of buyers and sellers. It operates at the local, national and international levels. The modern economy which uses the 'market' as the organizing principle has profit as the motive and continued growth as the goal. The positive value of the 'market' is in the decentralization of decisions and the freedom of individuals compared with centralization as in a planned economy. It also leads to a diversification of choice for the consumer, where production is linked with supply and demand. For example, there are 5,000 different categories of wool recognized by the traders in the wool market according to length of fibre, tensile strength, elasticity, susceptibility to dyes and so on. In a centrally planned economy this qualitative different information is suppressed. The officials organizing the economy have no means of monitoring consumer requirements. Wool is a homogenous material. A similar situation exists when one company takes over the market of a particular product: consumer choice is reduced as there are no other competitors and no incentives to make such a choice available. The increasing role of multi-nationals in the global economy is such that the supposed 'free' choice of a market economy is being distorted by their influence. The positive value of the 'market' is that it is sensitive to changing circumstances and is more participatory in that the users decide through their choices which product will be produced.

The damage done to the environment is not always monitored adequately in calculations of overall market cost of a process. This is particularly important for multi-nationals which, by their sheer size, have a relatively greater influence in environmental terms. A working approach tends to be what can be done within the *legal limits* of the country concerned, rather than a realistic estimate of the actual cost of environmental damage. In this way the market economy tends to ignore the real costs of environmental damage. This process becomes more complicated once the damage is at a site far removed from the site of production, as in the generation of gases which lead to acid rain, for example.

- Design a questionnaire that could be given to multi-national organizations in order to monitor the way their processes lead to environmental damage. Do you think that it will be feasible to arrive at international legal consensus?

- How far is the above tendency for damage to the environment to be ignored in economic terms applicable to economic structures other than a market economy, such as the centralized economy of the former Eastern block?

The creation of the 'market' had far reaching social and ecological consequences which were initially hidden from view. The 'market' required the transformation of nature to land, life into labour and inheritance into capital. Land was abstracted from the totality of the natural world and treated as an exchangeable commodity. Work time or labour was abstracted out of life and treated as a commodity to be valued and exchanged according to supply and demand. However, labour is not just a commodity like any other and wages need to be kept above a certain minimum. Again, the abstraction of land as a resource makes concern for the overall biosphere peripheral to land economics, and the latter peripheral to economics in general.

- Do you think that the market economy is ethically neutral? Is it the best system available or should we look for alternatives?

There has been relatively little perception amongst economists who advocate a market economy of the *ecological limits* to economic growth. Further, the market economy leaves out of its calculations those who do not contribute to the market, an issue which I raised in 3(b) above. Many today believe that these are limitations of the market economy which have to be accepted as a pre-condition for the progress that is possible within our present society. Inequality is not viewed as injustice because there is no intention that the poor will suffer. They argue that the poor sector can be catered for through charities and social benefits. The underlying assumption is that economic growth amounts to progress.

Consider the example of the mine closures in the UK in 1992. The closures were prompted by the market no longer seeming to require coal at high cost compared with North Sea gas to generate electricity. Yet there was little consideration of the potential damage to the social structure of the mining community. On the surface it might appear to be fostering environmental concern by promoting the use of 'cleaner' North Sea gas compared with coal. However, the damage to the environment is still present through the lack of real consideration of the potential of rigs and other appliances for environmental damage in addition to that caused by burning fuels.

- Should the market be allowed to set the alternative means of energy production? What kind of value can be given to safeguarding a human community? What ethical issues are raised?

The collapse of the economic state systems in Eastern Europe has fostered a sense of resignation that there is no real alternative to the market economy. Yet the parallel rise in unemployment which has come as part of the market economy package is now putting considerable strain on those nations in the transition phase from communism to democracy. The collapse of the Berlin wall led to widespread jubilation at the time as a new stage in the history of a re-united Germany. However, the transition has brought with it new tensions and difficulties. The securities of the old system begin to seem like a welcome alternative to the ambiguities of the new market economy. Unemployment, polarization of wealth and poverty, lack of state support for marginalized groups are all symptomatic of the new system which promises more than it delivers. For others, the transition to the Western model has led to profound individual freedom of expression and possibilities for new careers and opportunities.

• Set up a role play between a middle-aged woman from the former East Berlin who has lost her job in the unification of Germany, a man from the former Eastern sector who has found opportunities for study at a university in the West, a Turkish migrant worker, an unemployed factory worker from former West Berlin seeking employment, and a social worker from West Berlin who is actively engaged in political issues and whose family was reunited by the changes. How do you think each person can come to terms with the difference between the dream of a reunited Germany and the harsh realities of this change?

The gross national product (GNP), an indicator of a nation's wealth, measures gross output. The damage to the environment involved in producing manufactured goods, food, raw resources is not measured. The idea that there are ecological limits to growth is forcing economists to consider an alternative steady-state economics which is not directed towards limitless expansion. Whether it is possible for this shift to be incorporated into the market economy system is a matter for debate which I will take up under section (d) below.

(d) Free trade

The 'market' is also closely linked with the idea of 'free trade' between nations. The General Agreement on Tariffs and Free Trade (GATT) was founded within the UN in 1948 with the aim of encouraging free trade between nations through low tariffs, abolitions of quotas and curbs on subsidies. The ideal of free trade is argued as follows. If one nation lying in the tropics produces an abundance of bananas but no apples or pears, while another in the temperate zone produces apples and pears but no bananas and mangos, then there are obvious advantages to both in exchange. Economists do not try to prove this. What economists try to prove is that even when both nations can produce the goods in question, it is to their advantage to specialize and exchange. Since both nations have the ability to produce the raw materials, there might appear to be little incentive for trade. Economists introduced the idea that one of the nations will be able to produce the goods more cheaply than the other and so will be in what they call a *comparative advantage*. As long as both countries have different comparative advantages of one product, exchange between them can take place. For example, Portugal is at a comparative advantage over the UK in wine production. It is worth while exchanging wine for cloth if it costs Portugal more to produce cloth compared with wine and if it costs the UK more to produce wine than cloth.

Unfortunately the above conditions are often not met. If Portugal put all of its capital into wine production, soon the market would be satiated and profits would decline. New areas of investment in cloth manufacture outside the UK could put the cloth makers in the UK out of business. In other words, where one country has the comparative advantage for a time, this may not last where newer, cheaper means of production arise elsewhere. This is particularly significant in those countries such as the UK where the long history of industrialization has left a legacy of older, less efficient machinery. Unemployment rises in the country where the comparative advantage is lost. National boundaries inhibit the flow of labour so that the opportunities for employment decline in those countries where investments are low. The law of the market and free trade appears more like the 'survival of the fittest'.

- Car manufacturing in Japan has superseded that in the UK. discuss the implications for car assembly workers in the UK.

- Can you think of some other examples of manufacturing which has increased in one country at the expense of employment in another country?

New opportunities for employment depend on capital investment in order to keep abreast of new means of production. The relative comparative advantage will also depend on the availability of 'cheap labour'. The overall result of free trade is power for individual capitalists who no longer see the national community as their context. The free market trader in a cosmopolitan world easily loses touch with community obligations. The shift required is one towards a more balanced trade where there are rules imposed to protect the community interest. The ideal of *free trade* becomes modified in the light of the effects on the community, including the ecological community. The GATT agreements frequently reach deadlock over the need for some nations to subsidize particular communities. For example, in November 1992 the European Community negotiator agreed to scale down farm subsidies, but the French government refused to give their support. It also accounts for the fierce resistance to a reduction in agricultural subsidies by the French farming community. GATT may also become significant ecologically in its policy to resist the use of specific labels such as 'dolphin-friendly' tuna, in that it views such labels as a barrier to trade. The conflict is now between the consumer and free trade, rather than simply protecting the rights of individual communities which produce the goods.

• Discuss alternative means of exchange of goods between nations, such as a return to a barter system. What are the advantages and disadvantages?

The current crisis in Third World debt which has emerged as a result of the system of free trade has had devastating ecological and social consequences. Free trade, then, is often a mixed blessing. I raised this issue in the earlier chapters on Practical Issues of Environmental Concern and Ecology and Ethics.

4. Alternative socio-political models

(a) Transformation

There are those for whom the project of modernity should not be abandoned, but reformed in the light of the current awareness of ecological issues. This would not mean the rejection of technology, but the development of alternative technology which consumes *less* energy and is *less* polluting.

- What are some of the advantages of adopting a stance which works for the transformation of present systems?

An alternative technology would include ecological considerations in planning and management. However, the basic philosophy of expansion would remain intact. The problem remains as to how far we can allow such expansion to continue. The situation is ambiguous with respect to the poorer nations. Should different levels of expansion operate in different places? The problem is that while there is still a fundamental attitude of expansionism and of treating nature as an economic resource, the ecological crisis is delayed, but its potential impact is not weakened.

- What would be the long-term effect of keeping an expansionist policy intact? Who should decide the limits of expansion?

(b) Radical action/alternative communities

The opposite extreme to a conservative preservation of the status quo is to press for a complete restructuring of society which focusses on perceiving ourselves as members of a community. Those who hold this view believe that working to transform the system in the manner described above is a step in the right direction, but does not go nearly far enough. *All* the cosmos is part of this larger community. According to this philosophy the economic system would have to take account of the *ecological* limits to expansion. In practice this implies steady-state economic growth, rather than expansionism as discussed above. The damage done to our natural environment becomes *equivalent*, in terms of political priorities, to damage done to ourselves. This would give rise to new legislation which will protect the environment and give special 'rights' to non-humans.

- What practical steps could governments take to legislate for the protection of the environment?

The movement of radical action is in sympathy with the more radical women's movement that I raised in an earlier chapter on Women and Christian Community'. It is also in line with the 'deep ecology' philosophy which I mentioned in the chapters on Ethics and Gaia. The very different experience of women in the workplace is more likely to be taken into account in a social structure that is not bent on production and expansion. The link between the women's movement and the ecological movement with their mutual emphasis on community concerns shows the positive contribution of women to the field of ecological politics. The women's movement seems to be right in its insistence that the application of more technology is, at best, a partial remedy for dealing with the damage we have caused to the natural environment. Nonetheless, the politics of the radical women's movement is still primarily directed towards challenging male dominance in society, which is then linked with challenging exploitation of the earth.

- Set up a debate between those in favour of transformation and those in favour of radical action.

One of the predicaments of modern society is the remoteness of institutionalized political structures. Even the revolutionary movements themselves can become, in sociological jargon, 'routinized' into cumbersome bureaucratic organizations which develop the trappings of a new status quo. By this I mean that even the most radical groups, in the end, tend to become established and settled. The original drive and vision for radical change is lost in the new established structures. The overall result may be only a slight improvement on the earlier structure prior to the 'revolution'. I mentioned in an earlier section that many feel alienated from political structures of any kind. The alienation stems from a sense of remoteness of the organization to the real, practical concerns of the people concerned. There seems to be an impersonal belief system which is out of touch with grass roots action and interaction. The development of structures like family, church, neighbourhood and voluntary organization offsets the felt alienation against an impersonal faith in either left or right-wing political systems. They are not established political groups, yet they are a means for a community to find identity.

- Do you think that all churches can act to foster community spirit? What are the particular temptations for (i) an established church? (ii) a radical free church?

The concept of *intermediate* technology is the return to local production by those at the site of the raw materials. It is preferable to large-scale mass production where human 'labour' is treated as a commodity to be dispensed with depending on market forces. Intermediate technology is conducive to decentralization, compatible with ecology and allows for limited use of scarce resources. Large-scale mass production, on the other hand, is inherently violent and ecologically damaging, even though it seems to be more cost effective. The economic advantage to the nation in more efficient production of goods in factories has to be offset against the greater ecological damage. Schumacher pioneered ideas about the social advantage of small community sites of production in his book *Small is Beautiful*.[2] The idea of intermediate technology is becoming more popular in the poorer countries of the world where the capital investment required for large-scale mass production is not forthcoming. It is related to the idea of *alternative* technology, which is a more efficient means of energy production. For particular examples of alternative technology, see chapter 1 on 'Practical Issues of Environmental Concern'. Intermediate technology will often use *local* energy sources such as wind power. Hence, an intermediate technology project can include the use of alternative technology.

- Imagine that you are setting up a community which lived according to ecological principles. Discuss the extent of the commitment to green policies. Areas under discussion would be:
    Fund raising for the project
    Transport of members of the community
    Use of foodstuffs and land for home-produced
        vegetables
    Policies in the purchase of housing

Inclusion of those with learning difficulties or disadvantaged in other ways.

- Write out a list of the house 'rules' at the management level and the individual level which emerge from this discussion.

While the existence of ecologically sustainable communities will not create an alternative society, they challenge the credibility of the dominant myth of progress which has become one of the idols of our time. Nonetheless, there are also relatively few communities which have as their aim an ecologically acceptable lifestyle even though they have opted out of the market economy system. (For a further discussion of the ideal of community see chapter 4 on Ecology, Women and Christian Community.)

- Do you think that it is ever possible to live as a radical ecological community within a market economy? What contribution can these communities make to the wider society? What are their drawbacks?

- How do you think a sense of community can inform the way we conduct politics and economics?

9

Future Directives for an Ecological Theology

Ecological theology is still in its infancy compared with the more established fields of contemporary theology, such as liberation theology or feminist theology. I have tried in this book to offer some first steps towards making different areas of theological studies more aware of the relevance and significance of green issues as a theme for orientation and reflection. In this chapter I intend to point to new approaches that could be used which connect different themes in this handbook. It is not intended to be an exhaustive summary of what has gone before, but to show how some themes lend themselves to discussion across different subject disciplines. A holistic approach which draws out the interconnectedness between different disciplines within Christian theology is preliminary to a wider dialogue with other religious or secular fields. I intend to give four examples of overlapping themes, though users of this handbook may like to explore other topics that I have indicated at the end of this chapter.

The topics under discussion here are:

1. Sustainable development
2. The place of humankind in creation
3. Ecology and the freedom of the individual
4. Ecological spirituality

These topics are also interrelated, as I hope to clarify below.

1. Sustainable development

One of the core problems that this book has addressed is the environmental stress associated with poverty and land use. An enhanced ecological awareness includes a greater sensitivity to justice within the human community and the way this impinges on the human and non-human ecology of a particular area. Many of the environmental pressures have global consequences as I noted at the start of this book. The historical reasons for this stress are connected with the expansion of Europe, though the modern context is complicated by military and political instability in the Third World and Eastern Europe. Even these distinctions may not be helpful because of the diversities of lifestyles within both the rich nations of the North and the poorer nations of the South.

Practical steps towards the resolution of this issue require considerable sacrifice on behalf of the richer nations and communities. The idea of *development* used to be identified with the import of Western technology and culture. Today aid agencies are concerned to give land and power back to those marginalized by commercial farming. While sustainability has become a catchword in recent years, especially since the Rio conference, the basic idea of sustainability is too vague to implement ecologically based principles. Sustainability on its own merely stipulates that resources used have to be within those available in order to support the next generation. It could, in theory, encourage an artificial expansion in one region at the expense of another region. In other words we need to add the principles of *global justice* and *ecological responsibility* to sustainable development. An example of this idea of *sustainable* development that is *ecologically* efficient is the replacement of luxury cash crops for Western markets by more basic food crops, such as maize, millet etc.

Another example nearer to home is the idea of community forests first launched by the Forestry Commission in 1989. There are twelve planning developments in the UK which are designed to create forests which have a multiple purpose on the outskirts of major towns and cities in England and Wales. The role of community forests includes timber production, leisure and recreation. The idea is primarily to convert wasteland 'back to life', where the 'forest' consists of a network of community woodlands (broadleaved) along with farmland, heathland and other features such as meadows and lakes. According to the planning department of Middlesbrough Borough Council, the Cleveland Community Forest is 'to be a conservation focus as part of a sustainable society'. The intention is to increase the forest cover in the area from 6–7% in 1992 to 30% by 2030.

- The forest allows for regeneration of forest cover with associated beneficial effects such as providing new environments for wildlife and helping to offset the greenhouse effect.

  But is the forest necessarily an ecologically better use of land compared with 'greenbelt' countryside?

- Those who currently own land will welcome the proposal as they will be able to diversify and become involved as volunteers in the replanting schemes.

  But will the farmers agree to replant their land? Will the development have an overall detrimental effect on the area by encouraging tourism and possible vandalism? Who will benefit from the scheme?

The biblical principle of justice for the poor and marginalized is the basis for ecologically sound sustainable development. The Old Testament also links the idea of God's blessing of the people with blessing the land. If we treat the land with respect through practical steps such as careful management of woodland schemes, along with adequate crop rotation and awareness of the potential ecological risks in use of pesticides and fertilizers, we can expect a sense of God's blessing and approval.

There are also links between questions of justice, peace and environment. Consider the following example of the way military intervention in the Marshall Islands had a devastating effect on the environment and the society and culture of these islands.

At the Manila World Council of Churches (WCC) consultation on New Technology, Work and the Environment in January

1986, Darlene Keju-Johnson described what it was like to grow up in the Marshall Islands:

> I grew up on an island 300 miles downwind of Bikini Atoll. As a child I remember seeing the flash from one of the many tests. Like many other Marshallese I have fears about my health. Already I have had surgery to remove two tumours, and I have more that must be removed . . . Our fish are increasingly poisonous, and our arrowroot, a staple food for Marshallese (like a potato), has completely disappeared from the northern islands . . . People have a fear that almost every health problem is caused by radiation. It is becoming a big psychological problem for Marshallese people . . . Our own Marshallese doctors have no knowledge of radiation – they don't understand the health problems that result from radioactivity. So we have to rely on US government doctors who tell us not to worry, that everything is OK – even when we know it is not . . . We've had sixty-six atomic and hydrogen bombs dropped on our islands by the USA; six islands have been blown off the face of the earth.[1]

This story is a moving account of the suffering and oppression of a people and their land for the sake of a grasping after military supremacy. The harsh realities of the ecological crisis have forced us to reconsider our attitudes to the environment and the possible roots of these attitudes. A change in attitude implies a turning away to a different way of life, or *metanoia*.

• What ecological issues are raised through the use of conventional weapons and nuclear weapons? Should environmental ethics be included in political decisions about whether to take up arms?

Responsible sustainable development implies, then, a *global* perspective on the consequences of particular political decisions. The earth is able to support the total human population, but at a cost of readjustment of priorities and lifestyles. For the poorer peoples this means access to basic education, employment and health care within the context of their particular culture. In rural areas it includes a secure access to land as a necessary prerequisite to subsistence farming. For the wealthier peoples the readjustment is away from consumerism to the adoption of simpler lifestyles. I have given some practical suggestions as to how lifestyles can become more self-consciously ecological in the Appendix *What on Earth Can I Do?*

The challenge to technology is to become more aware of the ecological consequences of its use. Wealthier nations are, to some extent, locked irreversibly into the use of highly sophisticated industrial equipment producing toxic and pollutant waste. The expense of introducing more technology to minimize pollution is too great for those poorer countries struggling to expand industrially. The alienation felt between human beings and their own material inventions is part of a deeper alienation between human beings and 'nature'. One of the tasks of contemporary theology is to remind us of our connectedness with the earth and the interdependence between material existence and human life. The urbanization of human communities has subtly changed the rural patterns of life which fostered a close alliance with the natural world.

- Discuss different ways in which those in urban communities can become more aware of the natural world. Do you think that fostering 'wilderness' experiences promotes romantic escapism?

2. The place of humankind in creation

What is the relationship between God and creation? Traditional theology has stressed the idea of God as Lord of creation, ruling over the world rather like a beneficent monarch. According to this view the world is created out of nothing through the activity of divine agency. As humans made in the image of God our task becomes that of imitation of divine kingship. We are subservient to the King of the Universe and treat the world accordingly as stewards of creation.

- Discuss the relationship between our concept of God and our concept of ourselves. Is the connection unique to Christianity?

There are some theologians who are concerned that this approach is still too anthropocentric. It still encourages us to treat creation as resources to be managed for human benefit. More radical theologians argue that the adoption of a lifestyle which respects and loves creation for its own sake, quite apart from human self-interest, is part of what it means to be made in the image of God. Now the very image of God is transformed so that there is an even greater identification between God and creation: the world becomes God's body. One of the advantages of this view is that it promotes our sense of re-connectedness with nature. It seems to offer a way out of the sense of imprisonment by a technological impersonal culture. The difficulty is in conceiving in what sense God can be considered one who has power over creation. If God is powerless, then creation seems to be subject to chance alone. It is also very close to the idea of *pantheism*, which makes no distinction between God and creation.

A modified form of pantheism, known as *panentheism*, still allows for a distinction between God and the world. It seems to me to offer the most fruitful alternative available. It allows for a sense of the traditional understanding of the Lordship of God, yet is a Lordship based on the love of God, rather than the will to power. The biblical theme of the love of God for creation is particularly strong in wisdom literature, such as Psalm 104, which speaks of the relationship of joy between God and creation. As such it can encourage a love of humanity for creation as those made in God's image.

Pantheism, that is a close identification of God with the world, is also problematic when it comes to practical Christian ethics. How are we to decide in complex situations where the interests of one particular group or species clashes with another? The *Gaia* hypothesis is often used as a scientific basis in support of 'deep ecology'. However, if humans become rather like a 'cancer' on the planet, which is the opinion of some 'deep ecologists', the survival of any species which is deemed out of phase with continued planetary existence would be in queston. The logical scenario would be to eliminate those human populations which are causing the most obvious stress to the planet.

• How far is there evidence for a link between different religious beliefs in faiths other than Christianity and their treatment of nature?

The ethical demand is for a greater sense of basic equality between humans, while encouraging cultural diversity at local and national levels. This basic equality in practice means economic and political freedom for all to adopt a lifestyle that is in tune with the environment. The growth in human community life away from the misery of poverty and the emptiness of consumerism is a common goal regardless of the particular culture in question. It need not lead to a total rejection of technology, but *appropriate* use of technology. Instead of allowing ourselves to be the slaves of technology, we can make it our servant if we use it wisely, with due regard to its effects on the environment.

The market economy encourages an attitude to other people and nature on the basis of their value in terms of monetary resources. A Christian ethic roots the value of all creatures in the love of God, while recognizing the special value of all humankind made in God's image. This speaks against the injustice between peoples, while retaining a sense of realism in practical agriculture and technology. A Christian ethic demands, then, a sense of responsibility for action once we recognize our place in creation.

3. Ecology and the freedom of the individual

One of the most important insights of Enlightenment thought was to stress the value of individual insights and the human dignity of each and every person. A negative consequence is an individualism which refuses to consider the wider needs of the whole community. The challenge of ecological thinking is to temper selfish aspects of individualism without losing a sense of respect for the individual. I mentioned *metanoia* in the context of sustainable development. Turning away from individualism is one of the first steps towards achieving the end of responsible sustainability. The tension between individual convenience and corporate responsibility is felt in a number of areas. I will highlight three areas for discussion.

(a) Public and private transport

There is no doubt that certainly in the UK and Europe there has been a boom in private ownership of cars in the last half century. There has also been a considerable expansion in access to public transport, allowing for much greater international contact. The development of road transport in Germany and the UK seems to have developed haphazardly through isolated decisions of particular interest groups.[2] It seems that decisions have been made without adequate reference to the environmental consequences of mass transport. The positive value of private motoring is the freedom of movement of individuals and their families, security for travellers, greater mobility for those who are physically handicapped, ease of distribution of goods. The negative effects include the serious injuries and loss of life in road accidents. There are 3,500 road deaths in Britain each year. There is also a rise in demand of non-renewable energy with associated pollution and demand for parking space. The motor cars themselves contain materials that are not easily recycled. There is also a rise in level of noise pollution and consequent loss in quality of life.

- Set up a debate between those who argue for and against mass transport. What conclusions do you reach?

One of the difficulties is that the full extent of the consequences of mass transport were not necessarily known either by the public or by those who pressed for increased expansion. An important ethical question is: Whose interests does this policy serve? What about those who cannot articulate their concerns? This latter category would include the non-human species adversely affected. One way of trying to encourage the greater development of public transport is through the introduction of an ecological road tax. The proceeds of this tax would pay for public transport. There could also be a ban on freight transport by road. Another idea is the introduction of a specified charge depending on the number of kilometres travelled.

- Discuss the above proposals, that is the introduction of an ecological road tax, a ban on freight road transport and a penalty for those making the longest journeys. Do you think these proposals should be enforced by law? Do the benefits outweigh the infringement of freedom of the individual?

(b) Exploitation and preservation

One of the traditional concerns of conservation groups has been the preservation of species and communities. So far in this book I have mentioned the example of tropical rain forests as an area for debate. Is the opposite of preservation exploitation, or is there a means of achieving responsible change? It is clear that moves to try and *recreate* the 'original' landscape are often naive and romantic. One example is the proposed reintroduction of wolves into the Scottish forests. Although these creatures were part of the original woodland, they are not the only species whose population has changed as a result of human activity. Furthermore, worldwide, wolves are not an endangered species. Their effects on the farming communities on the fringes of the forest could be devastating. Other examples include mining projects where the developers claim that following the exhaustion of the mines the land will be 'restored' for recreational use. In these cases an 'artificial' natural landscape replaces the original one.

- Do we have a right to request the Third World to preserve the rain forests when all of our original forests have disappeared? Do you think that attempts to restore the original ecology of the UK are naive?

- Discuss the overall economic benefits of mining or other industrial activity. Do you think that land restoration justifies the original exploitation?

Another key question is raised by leaving areas untouched as 'wilderness' regions for recreation and relaxation. In earlier centuries we tended to see the natural world as a threat to organized existence. Our task was to tame 'wild' nature and to transform it for our own ends. In time this task took on a more sinister note. The popular practice of gardening seems like an innocuous pastime. Individuals have the freedom to change their landscape to fit their own particular taste and interest. However, the urge to control nature gradually became less innocent and developed into the means of acquiring gain through exploitation. The expanding urban communities have led to a greater detachment of humans from the natural world, as I mentioned earlier. The need to experience the wilderness as something positive was only really possible once nature could be exploited and dominated by human interest. It led, then, to a freedom from the fear of nature. But does the renewed contact with the natural wilderness areas lead to a greater connectedness with the earth? Or is it merely felt as a means for personal and psychological renewal in order to fulfill the pressurized and busy lifestyles of twentieth-century humanity?

- Discuss the advantages of wilderness preservation. Do you think it leads to a romantic escapism?

(c) Population

The population question is an enormous issue which I will touch on briefly here in order to highlight the conflict it raises between ecology and freedom of the individual. It is well known that in China births are artificially restricted by government policies. In the poorer communities of the world, which are not subject to these restrictions, children are viewed as an investment in the future. There is a high mortality rate and those children who survive are expected to care for their parents in old age. The link between population growth and ecological pressure is well established. Third World cities are expanding at the fastest rate in what seems like a runaway growth. But do those in the richer countries have a right to cast blame on those in the Third World who are having large families when they do not face the same issues of survival? Furthermore, the overall ecological pressure caused by the consumerism of an individual in the Western world far outweighs that of an individual living a simple lifestyle in the Third World. The population explosion in the Third World nonetheless presents an enormous problem for those countries facing widespread malnutrition and shrinking resources.

- The enforced control of women's fertility is one answer to the population expansion problem. Discuss the ethical issues raised by this form of exploitation.

One of the main issues raised by the population issue is how to tackle the root causes of poverty. There is a need for positive discrimination in favour of women to ensure adequate provision of food, healthcare and education and employment.

A concern for churches is how far particular birth control policies really take into account the global ecological issues and the strain that overpopulation is making on the earth. Statements from the Roman Catholic Church which have implied that the population question is not a serious threat have alienated those who are aware of the potential unsustainability of the current global population expansion.[3] The statement by the Pope in the document *Humanae Vitae* that 'each and every marriage act must remain open to the transmission of life' reaffirmed the traditional teaching of the Roman Catholic Church on contraception. This document has led to a huge controversy among priests and lay members. Even though it carries the personal authority of the Pope, many Catholics believe that it is not possible to adhere to the teaching. In this case the freedom of the individual seems to have been infringed by an overzealous focus on intimate practices within relationships which were outside the experience of the celibate authorities. Those who choose to dissent could do so on the basis that the faithful also have a contribution to make to the teaching of the church. Furthermore, *Humanae Vitae* is not an infallible statement. The teaching it contains is reformable.

- Discuss the ethical issues raised by the ban on artificial means of birth control in *Humanae Vitae*. What was the original intention of this ban? Does this represent an unacceptable infringement of the freedom of the individual?

4. Ecological spirituality

The prayer life of the early church was quite unselfconscious about its rootedness in creation themes. I have drawn particularly on the example of the Celtic church in this respect earlier in this book. An inner spiritual transformation which recognizes the value of creation fosters responsible action. One fundamental Christian basis for this spirituality lies in a deeper appreciation of the Trinitarian life of God. God as fully incarnate in Christ confirms the material worth of creation. The close communion between Father and Son and Spirit shows how we become closer to God through sharing in the dynamic relationships of the Trinity. Our prayer becomes caught up into the eternal prayer of the Godhead.

Prayer as communion with God becomes expressed through the liturgical life of the church. In times when we are reminded of the material worth of creation, prayer becomes a fellowship with all living creatures. Prayer becomes strength to persist in the midst of the world's conflicts and contradictions.

- Discuss ways in which prayer on behalf of all creation can become a practical reality. What are the possible dangers of this approach?

A prayer rooted in the love of God and creation becomes more real if it is also part of the faith of the church. This faith has its foundations in the life of the first Christian communities who tried to express their faith by living in obedience to the Spirit of God. This Holy Spirit gave them discernment to challenge those political structures which openly suppressed the Christian way. This readiness to challenge is part of what it means to live out an authentic Christian existence. For an ecological ethic this means in practice standing against political action which ignores environmental issues. While the practical results of such witness may be disappointing, as at the Earth Summit in Rio in July 1992, there is still value in the church maintaining its role as witness to Christian ethical principles.

An ecologically sensitive spirituality is also inclusive of insights from those who are marginalized from decision making, especially those who have been rendered powerless because of their race and/or gender. I am talking here about those who are on the *margins* of society. Those who are not in positions of particular influence in church or society can still make their voice heard through appropriate channels. However, those who are on the margins in a democratic society or those who are oppressed in an autocratic society are effectively 'voiceless'. In most cases women across the globe have been discriminated against in decision-making. The sensitivity of women to green issues means that ecological spirituality is active and flourishing in many women's groups. However, not everyone will be comfortable with the particular form of green spirituality that takes shape when it emerges from the exclusive experience of women. Some feminists have included all those who are oppressed as part of the group from which they wish to speak.

• Is a focus on the marginalized and oppressed as a source of inspiration overly romantic? Do you think that others who are well educated can ever really speak on their behalf?

A holistic approach which is genuine in its effort towards inter-connectedness seeks to engage in dialogue with those whose starting point and presuppositions are different. Mutual respect between different persons implies a willingness to listen and a readiness to hope that conflicts will be resolved.

The hope for the future encouraged by an ecological spirituality is one which is rooted in the biblical concept of *shalom*, or right relationships of justice and peace. The fragile reality of the ecological networks should remind us that this *shalom* is not something which is possible to achieve, but is a state of being where we are in communion with God, other human beings and nature. Hope for the future which is realistic is fully aware of the human responsibility awakened by the ecological crisis. A hope that God will somehow remedy whatever mess we make of the earth is facile because it refuses to acknowledge our human freedom and responsibility.

As free agents we are free to decide whether we act in such a way that is in tune with the earth. The pressures of consumerism and materialism may militate against a desire to become more ecological in our lifestyles. For the church to become true to herself she needs to resist such pressures and encourage her members to be more authentic in living out their thought through action. It is responsibility that is felt at individual, local and political levels of existence. One aim of this handbook is that it will help to begin the task of sharing this responsibility with other members of the Christian church. While our task as Christians is also to welcome those of other religions into the process of dialogue, we need to have some basis on which we can state the case for committed action from our own particular religious tradition.

- Does your church community adopt a form of ecological spirituality?

- Discuss an example of pollution in your local area. How does it impinge on biblical principles? ethical norms? political and economic questions?

- Why are efforts to engage in peacemaking so vital for planetary survival? Are we sometimes too quick to resort to military solutions?

- Can you think of examples in your own lifestyle where you become alienated from the material world through use of technology?

- What positive gifts of technology would you wish to encourage in our society?

Appendix 1

Liturgical Resources

Ideas to inspire your own liturgy

Many different groups have worked on their own liturgical materials the better to express ideas, beliefs and actions which are dear to their own hearts or to the heart of their worshipping community. For example, WWF has sponsored a number of new Christian liturgies for harvest, advent, Christmas and Easter, which have been developed with churches and cathedrals across the UK. It has also produced liturgies with other faith communities such as Buddhists, Muslims and Hindus. For further details or copies of the liturgies, please write to ICOREC, The Manchester Metropolitan University, 799 Wilmslow Road, Manchester M20 2RR, enclosing a SAE.

The sample which follows is from a harvest liturgy first used in Coventry Cathedral. It was taken from Creation Festival Liturgy, WWF/ICOREC *1988.*

Everyone stands
A reader, from the chancel lectern:
Father forgive us, for we knew not what we had done.

All: All we children of the Lord,
Cry aloud unto you Lord,
From ourselves free us to be your people,
Free us to praise and magnify you forever.

Reader: Creator of all, the hymn of creation has become the cry of the world. Like Adam and Eve in the garden, we hide ourselves in shame. Yet, just as you came to them and asked them lovingly, 'Where are you?', so in the Father who forgives you come to us today and lovingly, reconcilingly ask us, 'Where are you?'

We are here Lord, seeing ourselves as the centre of your world, and thus blind to the fact that you are the centre of all your creation.

All: Father forgive us for we knew not what we did.

Reader: We are here Lord, destroying in a few years the mighty works of aeons, so that we might be comfortable as we prepare our own Armageddon.

All: Father forgive, for we knew not what we did.

Reader: We are here Lord, knowing that you turned the tree of death into the tree of life, yet we smash to pieces the trees of life of our forests, using destructive powers to build our own cross of death.

All: Father forgive, for we knew not what we did.

Reader: We are here Lord, each in our own little world of creation. We have created the world of the church, of the home, of the workplace, of the environmental movement, as though there were no other worlds. From these little worlds reconcile us and draw us out into the new world which is your encompassing love.

All: All we children of the Lord,
Cry aloud unto our Lord,
From ourselves free us to be your people,
Free us to praise and magnify you forever.

Reader: We are here our brothers and sisters of the creation, with your life in our hands and your cries ringing in our ears. We who are part of you have set ourselves apart from you. We whom God loves as part of you, have taken that love as being only for us. Each day we take the final life of so many of your species which will never

be seen again. Each day we diminish your diversity and
in so doing are also diminished ourselves.

All: Brothers and sisters of creation, we know now what we
have done. Help us.

Reader: Our brothers and sisters of the creation, the mighty
trees, the broad oceans, the air, the earth, the creatures
of creation, forgive us and reconcile us to you. Let us
remake this world as a new world under the love and
compassion of the One who is the Beginning and the
End; who makes all things new; the Alpha and the
Omega.

All: All we children of creation,
Cry aloud unto our world,
From ourselves draw us out to be again a part of all
creation
That we may praise and magnify our Lord forever.

The Iona Community is one group which has developed new liturgies for many different occasions and causes. Their Celtic based material offers a host of new ideas and old resources, newly rediscovered. They can be contacted at the Iona Community, Isle of Iona, PA76 6SN, Scotland.

The three samples below are taken from The Iona Community Worship Book, *Wild Goose Publications/The Iona Community* 1991.

1. A Celtic Evening Liturgy

Opening Responses

Leader: Come to us this night, O God,

All: Come to us with light
              (*here a candle may be lit and placed centrally*)

Leader: Speak to us this night, O God,

All: Speak to us your truth.
              (*here a Bible may be placed centrally*)

Leader: Dwell with us this night, O God,

All: Dwell with us in love.
              (*here a cross may be placed centrally*)

Song

Prayer of Thanksgiving

Leader: Thanks be to you O Christ,

All: For the many gifts you have bestowed on us,
              Each day and night, each sea and land,
              Each weather fair, each calm, each wild.

Leader: Each night may we remember your mercy
given so gently and generously.

All: Each thing we have received, from you it came;
Each thing for which we hope, from your love it
Will come; each thing we enjoy, it is of your bounty,
Each thing we ask, comes of your disposing.

Leader: O God, from whom each thing that is, freely flows,

All: Grant that no tie over strict, no tie over dear,
May be between ourselves and this world.
Amen.

The Word of God

Leader: O God, as these words are read,

All: In our hearts may we feel your presence.

Reader: (a portion of scripture read clearly)

Song

Affirmation of Faith

All: We believe, O God of all Gods,
That you are the eternal God of life,
We believe, O God of all Gods,
That you are the eternal God of love.

Men: We believe, O God and Maker of all creation,
That you are the creator of the high heavens,
That you are the creator of the deep seas,
That you are the creator of the stable earth.

Women: We believe, O God of all the peoples,
That you created our souls and set their warp,
That you created our bodies and gave them breath,
That you made us in your own image.

All: We are giving you worship with our whole lives,

We are giving you assent with our whole power,
We are giving you our existence with our whole mind,
We are giving you kneeling with our whole desire.

Prayers of Concern

Leader: O Christ, kindle in our hearts within
A flame of love to our neighbour,
To our foes, to our friends, to our kindred all.

All: O Christ of the poor and the yearning,
From the humblest thing that lives
To the name that is highest of all,
Kindle in our hearts within
A flame of love.
*(Here a ring of votive candles may be lit around the
symbols, followed by a period of silence)*

OR

*(Each person may have a candle which will be lit from
neighbour to neighbour, followed by a period of
intercessions, freely spoken or unspoken)*
*(At the end of this time the following prayer will be
said:)*

Leader: We are placing our souls and our bodies
Under your guarding this night, O Christ.

All: O Son of the tears, of the wounds of the piercings,
May your cross this night be shielding all.

Song

Blessing

Leader: Be the great God between your shoulders
To protect you in your going and your coming;
Be the Son of Mary near your heart;
And be the perfect Spirit upon you pouring.

All: Amen.

2. *A Simple Evening Liturgy*

Opening Responses

Leader: Peace on each one who comes in need,
All: Peace on each one who comes in joy.

Leader: Peace on each one who offers prayers,

All: Peace on each one who offers song.

Leader: Peace of the Maker, Peace of the Son,

All: Peace of the Spirit, the Triune One.

Song

Prayer

Leader: O God, for your love for us, warm and brooding,
           which has brought us to birth and opened our eyes
           to the wonder and beauty of creation,

All: We give you thanks.

Leader: For your love for us, wild and freeing,
           which has awakened us to the energy of creation:
           to the sap that flows,
           the blood that pulses,
           the heart that sings,

All: We give you thanks.

Leader: For your love for us, compassionate and patient,
           which has carried us through our pain,
           wept beside us in our sin,
           and waited with us in our confusion,

All: We give you thanks.

Leader: For your love for us, strong and challenging,
which has called us to risk for you,
asked for the best in us,
and shown us how to serve,

All: We give you thanks.

Leader: O God we come to celebrate
that your Holy Spirit is present deep within us,
and at the heart of all life.
Forgive us when we forget your gift of love
made known to us in Jesus,
and draw us into your presence.

The Word of God

Song

Sharing of the Day *(The leader invites the company to share a
brief word or picture from today which is special in
some way)*

Prayer

*(Here is opportunity for prayers of concern, spoken or
unspoken – each prayer being followed by a chant)*
We bring to God someone whom we have met or
remembered today and for whom we want to pray
(Chant)
We bring to God someone who is hurting tonight and
needs our prayer
(Chant)
We bring to God a troubled situation in our world
tonight
(Chant)
We bring to God silently someone whom we find hard
to forgive or trust
(Chant)

We bring ourselves to God
that we might grow in generosity of spirit,
clarity of mind,
and warmth of affection.
(Chant)

Song

Closing Responses

Leader: O Trinity of Love,
You have been with us at the world's beginning,

All: Be with us till the world's end.

Leader: You have been with us at our life's shaping,

All: Be with us at our life's end.

Leader: You have been with us at the sun's rising,

All: Be with us till the day's end.
Amen.

Blessing

3. *A Creation Liturgy*

Opening Responses

Leader: Let the light fall warm and red on the rock,
            Let the birds sing their evening song
            And let God's people say Amen.

All: Amen.

Leader Let the tools be stored away,
            Let the work be over and done
            And let God's people say Amen.

All: Amen.

Leader: Let the flowers close and the stars appear,
            Let hearts be glad and minds be calm
            And let God's people say Amen.

All: Amen.

Song

Psalm or Reading *(concerning creation)*

Confession

Leader: O God, your fertile earth is slowly being stripped of its riches,

All: Open our eyes to see.

Leader: O God, your living waters are slowly being choked with chemicals.

All: Open our eyes to see.

Leader: O God, your clear air is slowly being filled with pollutants.

All: Open our eyes to see.

Leader: O God, your creatures are slowly dying and your people are suffering,

All: Open our eyes to see.

Leader: God our Maker, so move us by the wonder of creation,

All: That we repent and care more deeply.

Leader: So move us to grieve the loss of life,

All: That we learn to cherish and protect your world.

Chant

(during which there will be an action in which we commit ourselves to caring for God's earth or celebrate the goodness of God's earth)

Prayer of Thanksgiving/Intercession
Song

Closing Responses

Leader: This we know, the earth does not belong to us,

All: We belong to the earth.

Leader: This we know, all things are connected,

All: Like the blood that unites one family.

Leader: This we know, we did not weave the web of life,

All: We are merely a strand in it.

Leader: This we know, whatever we do to the web,

All: We do to ourselves.

Leader: Let us give thanks for the gift of creation,

All: Let us give thanks that all things
        hold together in Christ.

Blessing

Leader: Bless to us, O God,
        The moon that is above us,
        The earth that is beneath us,
        The friends who are around us,
        Your image deep within us,

All: Amen.

Additional material for the Creation Liturgy

Opening Responses *(alternative)*

Leader: Let the darkness of night surround us,
        Let light and warmth gather us
        And let God's people say Amen.

All: Amen.

Leader: Let the tools be stored away,
        Let the work be over and done
        And let God's people say Amen.

All: Amen.

Leader: Let the winds blow wild around us,
        But let hearts be glad and minds be calm
        And let God's people say Amen.

All: Amen.

Songs

Many And Great (Native Indian Tradition)
You Are Author And Lord Of Creation (Sara Shriste;
Nepal)
The Song Is Love
Sing Praise To God
Blessing And Honour
From Creation's Start
I Am For You
Lord Your Hands (Philippines)
Sing Out, Earth And Skies

Readings (*Scriptural*)

Psalms 19. 1–6; 23. 1–6; 29. 1–11; 46. 2–11;
65. 6–14; 67. 2–8; 72. 1–19; 80. 2–20; 84. 2–13;
85. 2–14; 89. 2–17; 96. 1–13; 97. 1–12; 100. 1–5;
104. 1–35; 131. 1–3; 147. 1–11; 148. 1–14.
Wisdom 7. 22–30; Job 38 & 39; Ecclesiasticus
42. 15–26; 43. 1–28.
Colossians 1. 15–20; 3. 11. Ephesians 1. 17–3.
Romans 8. 18–25.

Readings (*Mystics*)

From: *Meditations with Hildegarde of Bingen*

The earth is at the same time mother,
She is mother of all that is natural,
Mother of all that is human.

She is mother of all,
For contained in her are the seeds of all.

The earth of humankind contains all moistness,
All verdancy,
All germinating power.

It is in so many ways fruitful.

All creation comes from it
Yet it forms not only the basic raw material for
humankind,
But also the substance of the incarnation of God's Son.

From: *Meditations with Julian of Norwich*

I saw that God was everything that is good
And encouraging

God is our clothing
That wraps, clasps and encloses us
So as never to leave us.
God showed me in my palm
A little thing round as a ball
About the size of a hazelnut.

I looked at it with the eye of my understanding
And asked myself:
'What is this thing?'
And I was answered: 'It is everything that is created.'
I wondered how it could survive since it seemed so little
It could suddenly disintegrate into nothing.

The answer came: 'It endures and ever will endure,
Because God loves it.'

And so everything has being because of God's love.

From: *Meditations with Meister Eckhart*

Apprehend God in all things,
For God is in all things.

Every single creature is full of God
And is a book about God.

Every creature is a word of God.

If I spent enough time with the tiniest creature –
Even a caterpillar –
I would never have to prepare a sermon.
So full of God
Is every creature.

Prayers of Intercession

Prayer of Intercession based on Colossians 1. 15–20.

O Christ, your cross speaks both to us and to our world.
In your dying for us you accepted the pain and hurt
Of the whole of creation.
The arms of your cross stretch out across the
Broken world in reconciliation.

You have made peace with us.
Help us to make peace with you by sharing in your
Reconciling work.

May we recognize your spirit disturbing and
Challenging us to care for creation and for the
Poor who most feel the effects of its abuse.
O Christ, the whole of creation groans,
Set us free and make us whole.

Prayer of Intercession based on Ephesians 4. 7–16.

There is no pain in our hearts or in our planet
That you do not know,
For you have touched the lowest places on earth.

Teach us to grieve with you, O Christ, the loss of
all the beauty that is being killed.

There is no place in the heavens that cannot be
Touched by your resurrection presence,
For you fill all things.

Give us strength in your victory over death
To grow into your way of love,
Which does not despair but keeps sowing seeds of hope
And making signs of wholeness.

Under Christ's control all the different parts of
The body fit together and the whole body is held
Together by every joint with which it is provided.

Teach us to know our interconnectedness
With all things.
Teach us to grow with each other
And all living creatures through love.

Actions

*Some actions may be better placed after the prayers of
intercessions as with the following examples:*

*– People to light candles around a cross to signify
their share in reconciling creation to God (Colossians
1.15–20).*

*– People to add stones to a spiral of growth at the foot of
a cross committing themselves to growing in God's way
of love for creation and grieving the crucifixion of life on
earth (Ephesians 4. 7–16).*

Chants

Kindle A Flame
Dona Nobis Pacem In Terra (Give us peace on earth)
Kyrie Eleison (Lord have mercy: USSR or Ghana)
Mayenziwe (Your will be done: South Africa)
Your Kingdom Come O Lord (USSR)
Agios O Theos (Holy God have mercy: USSR)
Come Holy Spirit

Appendix 2

What on Earth Can I Do?

The environmental crisis often overwhelms people with the sheer complexity and diversity of the issues involved. The most common request ICOREC receives from religious groups is, What can I do? To answer this, it has produced, along with WWF, the following hints, suggestions and ideas. For those wishing to go further in practical projects, WWF and ICOREC have produced a Congregational Environmental Audit pack which enables you to assess ways in which your church buildings, clergy and members of the congregations can save fuel, aid reprocessing and make better use of the natural resources around you. This pack forms part of WWF and ICOREC's five-year scheme called 'Sacred Land – Rehallowing the environment of the UK'. This project runs until 2002 and is aimed at helping religious communities work on practical environmental projects from an avowedly religious perspective. For information on this pack contact ICOREC at The Manchester Metropolitan University, 799 Wilmslow Road, Manchester M20 2RR.

What on earth can I do?

WWF is working in Britain and in every continent to save endangered species and habitats. Our greatest global assets are being destroyed by mankind. Logging is destroying the rainforest, pollution from fossil fuel use is contributing to the greenhouse effect and the world's animals and forests are under threat. That is why we at WWF are appealing to people everywhere to become conservationists in their daily lives.

What on earth can I do? is your WWF guide to help the environment. The pressure on our planet has now become so great that a vital and urgent rethink into how we behave is now a necessity, not an option. Correct yesterday's mistakes today for a better tomorrow.

Wherever you are, whatever you are doing, you can all help the environment. Today we can all take responsibility for our planet.

RETHINK – AT HOME

As individuals we can all make small and simple changes in our lifestyle at home which can help the environment.

SAVE ENERGY AND COMBAT AIR POLLUTION

The coal, oil and gas burned in our homes and power stations give off carbon dioxide and other gases which contribute to the greenhouse effect and acid rain. By using less fuel, you can help combat these major environmental threats. Some of these measures may cost more initially but the reduction in running costs will save you money, often over very short periods.

- Ensure that lights and heating are switched off when rooms are not in use.

- Draught strip doors and windows and make sure you have at least 6″ of loft insulation.

- Lag your hot water tank and consider installing cavity wall insulation.

- If you need a new central heating boiler, fit a more energy efficient gas or oil condensing boiler.

- Fit thermostatic controls to your radiators and boiler, and a timer to your boiler to ensure that heat is provided only where and when it's needed. Put your central heating thermostat in the room where you spend most of your waking hours, and set it at around 18–20°C.

- Use compact fluorescent light bulbs instead of ordinary incandescent light bulbs. These use only a fraction of the energy of an ordinary light bulb, and although they are much more expensive to buy, they last eight times longer and will save you money because of reduced running costs.

- Buy energy efficient electrical appliances – ask the sales representative for the energy consumption figures.

- Send for WWF's new booklet. 'The Greenhouse Effect and You' for more details on how you can play your part in combatting the greenhouse effect.

IN THE KITCHEN

- In the fridge, instead of wrapping everything up in wasteful foil and plastic wrap, use containers.

- Where recycling facilities exist use them. Glass jars, bottles, newspapers, aluminium and steel cans can all be recycled. Every year in Britain we throw away 6 billion bottles and jars and 5 billion drink cans.

- Choose glass over plastic. Currently there are far more local authorities offering glass recycling facilities than plastic.

- Return milk bottles to the milkman or dairy.

- Your old fridges can be disposed of safely. Ask your local authority or the manufacturer to collect and recycle the CFC chemicals which each fridge contains.

SAVE THE RAINFOREST

- Wooden kitchen items and furniture often come from the rainforest. In 1988 the UK imported 1,375,000 cubic metres of tropical timber. Currently a very limited supply of sustainably produced tropical timber is available, therefore try and avoid tropical hardwoods unless it comes from a sustainable source and is labelled as such. Use temperate hard woods such as oak, ash and beech whenever you can, or use soft woods such as pine and larch.

WASTE NOT . . .

- Try to avoid throwing your waste down the sink.

- If you have a garden save your fruit and vegetable scraps and make a compost heap.

IN THE BATHROOM

- Over 300 million gallons of sewage is dumped in the sea every day. Some of this is raw sewage. Therefore avoid throwing anything down the toilet, including sanitary wear, cigarette butts, or plastic wrappings and labels. Sanitary wear can take 120 days to biodegrade and plastic wrappings do not biodegrade at all.

RETHINK – AT WORK

There is enormous wastage of paper and energy in the work place. Does your work place have an environmental policy? If not start one! Consider contacting your local council to see if they have any recycling facilities – you will be making a big contribution to the environment by starting to recycle today.

- In Britain every year we throw away paper and cardboard equivalent to 130 million trees. Save resources by recycling paper, cardboard, newspapers and introduce recycled paper into the work place.

- Save energy and thus reduce carbon dioxide. Turn off machines that you are not using, reduce unnecessary lighting and replace light bulbs with energy efficient ones.

- Is the workplace being cleaned with environmentally safe products?

- WWF supports the use of recycled paper because its manufacture uses considerably less energy and therefore produces less effluent than when paper is made from virgin pulp.

RETHINK – WHEN YOU TRAVEL

Do you need to drive the car as often? Over one million tonnes of carbon dioxide was released by our cars in Britain in 1988. This is a major contributing factor to the greenhouse effect. Vehicles also emit nitrogen oxides and hydrocarbons which contribute to acid rain and smog.

- Use the car only when absolutely necessary. By driving 30 miles less a week you will save £100 a year on fuel. Try walking or biking instead.

- Use public transport more often – and if the service is inadequate, make sure your MP or local authority knows about it.

- Consider sharing lifts with relatives and friends when driving to work or to the shops.

- Convert your car if suitable to unleaded petrol.

- Next time you buy a car, consider buying one with a 3 way catalytic converter which will reduce its emissions of nitrogen oxides and hydrocarbons by 90%.

- Recycle your engine oil (a garage can assist).

- Remember to drive slower. Reduced speeds mean less fuel is used and therefore less carbon dioxide is emitted.

RETHINK – WHEN YOU SHOP

Next time you go shopping take a moment to think of the effect your next purchase could have on the environment. There are safe alternatives to many of the products we buy today.

- Buy pump action sprays. Avoid aerosols. They use considerable amounts of energy to manufacture and even alternatives to CFCs contribute to the formation of low level ozone – a greenhouse gas.

- Buy recycled toilet tissue, stationery etc.

- If you can, buy in bulk – it saves packaging and money.

- Avoid products designed specifically for a short life span eg. many disposable items such as razors.

- Take your own shopping bag. Billions of non-recyclable or non-biodegradeable carrier bags are given away free and used only once.

RETHINK – ON THE COAST

Our coastline is very vulnerable. Take good care of it – it is the only one we have.

- Take your rubbish home. Around the world over 2 million seabirds and 100,000 sea mammals die annually trapped or injured by discarded rubbish.

- Dispose of your plastic multi-pack can holders sensibly. Hundreds of seabirds and marine mammals get caught in them and die.

- Respect your local marine environment – don't move rocks and stones in rockpools and avoid taking home shells and plants, however attractive they are.

- Water skiing, scuba diving and yachting can cause disturbance and even damage to marine life, such as nesting birds, seals with pups or families of dolphins. Where possible consult your local marine warden to ascertain particularly fragile areas which should be avoided.

- Anglers, please make sure you take home all your gear. Discarded hooks, weights, lines and nets can be hazardous to humans as well as wildlife.

- Don't stray off marked paths. It may be dangerous and could disturb sheltering wildlife or destroy plants.

RETHINK – IN THE GARDEN

- Start a compost heap in your garden with left-over fruit and vegetable scraps and garden debris. This compost will reduce the volume of household waste and can be used instead of peat.

- Don't buy peat. It is taken from peatlands and forms an irreplaceable habitat for many species of wildlife and plants. Since 1850 we have destroyed 96% of UK peatlands. Look for alternatives such as home made compost, or shredded bark.

- Choose organic fertilizers and try to avoid pesticides altogether.

- Encourage wildlife in your garden – put up nestboxes, build a hibernation spot with dead logs and leaves, encourage wildflowers to grow.

SPEAK UP FOR THE ENVIRONMENT!

- Write to your MP on local, national and international environmental issues that concern you.

- Campaign for better public transport and recycling facilities.

- Join an environmental group.

- Use less and tell others to conserve our precious resources as well.

- Spread the word amongst friends and colleagues.

Notes

1 Practical Issues of Environmental Concern

1. In ecology the carrying capacity of the environment refers to the maximum numbers of plants or animals that a particular area can support. It can refer to individual species or whole communities. When the carrying capacity is exceeded there are insufficient resources to sustain the population, which may be reduced by emigration, or reproductive failure or death caused by starvation or disease.

2. *Caring for the Earth: A Strategy for Sustainable Living*, IUCN/NUEP/WWF, Gland 1991

3. For specific stories of the struggle for land ownership see P. Vallely, *Promised Lands*, HarperCollins/Fount 1991

4. Land degradation can be caused by a number of factors including soil erosion, water logging, depletion of nutrients, deterioration of soil structure, deforestation, salinization, overgrazing and pollution.

2 Ecology and Biblical Studies

1. See, for example, F. Tipler, *The Physics of Immortality*, Macmillan 1994

2. L. White, 'The Historic Roots of our Ecologic Crisis', *Science*, 1967, 155, pp. 1203–1207. For a reply see J. Barr, 'Man and Nature: the Ecological Controversy and the Old Testament', *Bulletin of the John Rylands Library*, 1972, 55, pp. 9–32.

3. R. Carson, *Silent Spring*, Fawcett Crest 1962

3 Ecology and Celtic Christianity

1. For examples of how a modern writer has done just this see D. Adam, *Tides and Seasons* and *Power Lines*, SPCK 1989 and 1992

4   *Ecology, Women and Christian Community*

1. For a discussion of debates about this idea, see Elaine Graham, *Making the Difference: Gender, Personhood and Theology*, Mowbray 1995

6   *Ecology and Liturgy*

1. Ecumenical Patriarchate, *Orthodoxy and the Ecological Crisis*, WWF 1990, p. 5
2. See The St Hilda Community, *Women Included*, SPCK 1991
3. S. McFague, *Metaphorical Theology*, SCM Press 1983, pp. 13–14
4. Ecumenical Patriarchate, *Orthodoxy and the Ecological Crisis*, p. 5
5. For Celtic prayers written for contemporary use see E. de Waal and E. M. Allchin, *Threshold of Light: Prayers and Praises from the Celtic Tradition*, DLT 1986 and books by David Adam, for example *Tides and Seasons*, SPCK 1989
6. See, for example, B. Wren, *What Language Shall I Borrow?*, SCM Press 1989

8   *Ecology and Politics*

1. J. Moltmann, *Theology of Hope*, SCM Press 1967
2. E. Schumacher, *Small is Beautiful*, Abacus 1975

9   *Future Directives for an Ecological Theology*

1. Cited in D. Gosling, *A New Earth: Covenanting for Justice, Peace and the Integrity of Creation*, CCBI 1992, p. 32
2. See J. Rogerson, 'Theological Reflection on Transport Policy', *Theology in Green*, Autumn 1995, pp. 19–27
3. See S. McDonagh, *The Greening of the Church*, Orbis 1990, pp. 59–73

Bibliography

1 *Practical Issues of Environmental Concern*

IUCN/UNEP/WWF, *Caring for the Earth: A Strategy for Sustainable Living*, Gland 1991

B. Jackson, *Poverty and the Planet*, World Development Movement 1990

G. Lean, D. Henrichsen, and A. Markham, *WWF Atlas of the Environment*, Arrow/WWF 1990

2 *Ecology and Biblical Studies*

B. W. Anderson, *Creation in the Old Testament*, SPCK 1984

J. Rogerson, *Genesis 1–11*, JSOT Sheffield Academic Press 1991

3 *Ecology and Celtic Christianity*

C. Bamford and W. P. Marsh, *Celtic Christianity. Ecology and Holiness*, Floris Classics 1986

A. Carmichael, *Carmina Gadellica*, Floris Books 1992

E. de Waal, *A World Made Whole*, Harper Collins 1991

4 *Ecology, Women and Christian Community*

V. Fabella and E. Oduyoye (eds)., *With Passion and Compassion: Third World Women Doing Theology*, Orbis 1988

G. Jantzen, *God's World, God's Body*, Westminster 1984

R. Ruether, *Gaia & God; An Ecofeminist Theology of Earth Healing*, SCM Press 1993

5   Ecology and Ethics

R. Attfield, *The Ethics of Environmental Concern*, Blackwell 1983
D. Gosling, *A New Earth: Covenanting for Justice, Peace and the Integrity of Creation*, CCBI, Interchurch House 1992
K. Innes, *Caring for the Earth*, Grove Ethical Studies 66, 1991

6   Ecology and Liturgy

J. Morley (ed), *Bread of Tomorrow*, SPCK/Christian Aid 1992
G. Mueller-Nelson, *To Dance With God*, Paulist Press 1986
WWF, *Creation Festival Liturgy*, WWF/ICOREC 1988

7   Ecology and Gaia

C. Deane-Drummond, *Gaia and Green Ethics*, Grove Ethical Studies 88, 1993
J. Lovelock, *Gaia. A New Look at Life on Earth*, OUP 1979
E. Sahtouris, *Gaia: The Human Journey from Chaos to Cosmos*, Pocket Books 1989

8   Ecology and Politics

R. Ambler, *Global Theology*, SCM Press 1990
H. Daly, *Towards a Steady State Economy*, Freeman 1973
A. Dumas, *Political Theology and the Life of the Church* SCM Press 1978
J. Porritt, *Seeing Green*, Blackwell 1984

9   Future Directives for an Ecological Theology

E. Breuilly, C. Deane-Drummond and M. Palmer, *Faith in the Future*, HarperCollins 1991
E. Breuilly and M. Palmer (eds), *Christianity and Ecology*, Cassell/WWF 1992
D. Dorr, *The Social Justice Agenda*, Gill and Macmillan 1991

General

ACORA, *Faith in the Countryside*, Churchman Publishing Limited 1990

ACORA, *Short Report: Faith in the Countryside*, Churchman Publishing Limited 1990

R. Bauckham, *The Bible in Politics*, SPCK 1989

P. Bunyard and F. Morgan-Grenville (eds), *The Green Alternative: A Guide to Good Living*, Methuen 1987

J. Button, *How to be Green*, Century Hutchinson 1984

D. Carroll, *Towards a Story of the Earth*, Dominican Publications 1987

N. K. Chadwick, *The Age of the Saints in the Early Celtic Church*, OUP 1961

Church and Conservation Project, *The Living Churchyards: A DIY Information Pack*, CSV, London 1987 (This and audio visual material available from Development Officer, Church and Conservation Project, Arthur Rank Centre, Stoneleigh, Warwicks CV8 2LZ)

S. Clark, *How to Think About the Earth*, Mowbray 1993

S. Cleary, *Renewing the Earth: Development for a Sustainable Future*, CAFOD 1989

T. Cooper, *Green Christianity*, Hodder and Stoughton 1990

D. Dorr, *Integral Spirituality: Resources for Community, Justice, Peace and the Earth*, Gill and Macmillan 1990

W. Granberg-Michaelson (ed), *Tending the Garden: Essays on the Gospel and the Earth*, Eerdmans 1987

D. Hallman, *Ecotheology: Voices from South and North*, WCC, Geneva 1994

Hildegarde of Bingen, *Meditations with Hildegarde of Bingen*, tr. G. Uhlein, Bear and Company 1982

G. Jantzen, *God's World, God's Body*, Westminster 1984

U. King, *Feminist Theology from the Third World: A Reader*, SPCK 1994

G. Limouris (ed), *Justice, Peace and the Integrity of Creation*, WCC, Geneva 1990

A. Linzey, *Animal Theology*, SCM Press 1994

J. Lovelock, *The Ages of Gaia*, OUP 1989

S. McDonagh, *To Care for the Earth*, Chapman 1986

S. McFague, *The Body of God: An Ecological Theology*, SCM Press 1993

J. Moltmann, *God in Creation*, SCM Press 1985

J. Moltmann, *Creating a Just Future*, SCM Press 1989

E. Moltmann-Wendel, *A Land Flowing with Milk and Honey*, SCM Press 1986

R. F. Nash, *The Rights of Nature: A History of Environmental Ethics*, Princeton University Press 1986

J. Porritt, *Seeing Green*, Blackwell 1984

T. Roszak, *Person/Planet*, Granada 1981

H. P. Santmire, *The Travail of Nature*, Fortress Press 1985

E. Schememann, *Liturgy and Life: Christian Development through Liturgical Experience*, Department of Religious Education, Orthodox Church in America 1974

D. Soelle and S. Cloyes, *To Work and to Love: A Theology of Creation*, Fortress Press 1984

R. D. Sorrell, *St Francis of Assisi and Nature*, OUP 1988